LETTERHEADS

LETTERHEADS

A COLLECTION FROM AROUND THE WORLD.

Edited By Takenobu Igarashi

GRAPHIC-SHA

LETTERHEADS

世界のレターヘッド

五十嵐 威暢

グラフィック社

LETTERHEADS
A Collection from around the World

Editing and book conception	Takenobu Igarashi
Co-editing	Yoshiro Nakamura
Art direction	Takenobu Igarashi
Cover design	Tomoharu Terada
Layout	Yoshiro Nakamura
Photographs	Eigi Ina
	Roberto Carra (P106. 107)
Translations	NCB Development Center
Typesetting	Gaigo Printing, Ltd.
	Sanwa Typesetting Co., Ltd.
Printing and binding	Toppan Printing Co., Ltd.
Co-ordinating	Seiki Okuda
	Scott Brause

Edited by Takenobu Igarashi © 1986
Published by Graphic-sha Publishing Company Ltd. © 1986

ISBN4-7661-0408-0

Printed in Japan by Toppan Printing Co., Ltd.

First Edition December 1986

Graphic-sha Publishing Co., Ltd.
1-9-12 Kudan-kita Chiyoda-ku Tokyo 102 Japan
Phone 03-263-4310
Fax 03-263-5297
Telex J29877 Graphic

Abbreviations
AD — Art Director
D — Designer
A — Artist
C — Client

For some people there is nothing more difficult than writing a letter. In a situation where the correspondence is obligatory the task becomes all the more painful, even agonizing. And yet there is no pleasure like that of receiving a letter. Whether from a close friend or from someplace unknown and far away, the letter is invariably opened with excitement and anticipation. It cherishes a romantic image of a paper airship filled with messages, approaching from afar.

But every letter whether private or business, is first of all scrutinized for clues of its contents. Stamps, postmark, name and address of the receiver and the sender — these factors all contribute to an individual's interpretation in judging the importance of a letter. Here the type of writing paper and envelope, the writing tools, whether it be pen or brush, and even in the way the stamp is posted, will reflect upon the person of the sender. Every tangible element of the letter will leave an impression, leaving no room for insensitiveness. An effective and good letterhead design will encompass all of these points skillfully, conveying accurately the nature and personality of oneself or the company to the other party.

Around 1925 Herbert Bayer and Jan Tschichold began their ambitious attempts at experimenting freely with printing types and ruled lines, developing beautiful works of art that remain impressive today. Their typographical endeavours were furthered by German and Swiss designers, and eventually spread to other parts of the world.

The term "letterhead" evolved from the printed name and address, the information found at the "head" of the letter. Originally, design elements were kept to a minimum, and this can be said of today's letterhead designs as well. The selection of paper and typeface, and the layout of the name and address, are the essential elements of the designs.

With the coming of the sixties and great economic growth, letterhead designs began to flourish. Designers came forth with bold and vigorous new creations, and with the development of international communication, improved postal service, and the popularization of the typewriter, the concept of the letterhead found general acceptance. Particularly in America where stationery stores sell special envelopes, paper and cards for individual use, growth in this area has been exceptional. Nowadays it is hardly possible to begin a new business without first having an attractive letterhead in hand.

The vital function of a letter of an individual or of a company is to serve as a communicator of its character and philosophy. To put it another way, the design of the letterhead or envelope gives a clue of who and what the sender is, and what his work and way of thinking is like. The American designer Rod Dyer says "Stationery with a distinctive design stands out in the midst of the mountains of mail received daily. Even from across the room it will be distinguishable from the rest."

While stationery is normally something to be typed over, according to Don Weller, "even blank stationery has a certain beauty." The letterhead should be designed in such a way that it "stands by itself". When a letter is typed, it is rational — the typed letter being clear and neat, and easily readible in a short period of time. However, some typists prefer to innovate, to create letters with individuality. The work of the American designer April Greiman is an excellent example of this. She sets the letter paper in sideways or diagonally, making the body of her letter a part of the overall design. This may seem painstaking and no doubt unusual, but such a provocative style cannot fail to impart the message of her personality and philosophy. In her case the letterhead is expansively interpreted, exemplifying the emphasis placed on its unlimited possibilities.

Letterheads with enjoyable and appropriate designs can also alleviate much of the burden on those corresponding. The typewriter and word processor are here to stay and the need for incorporating innovative writing paper is a reality. Certain concepts are basic. For example, in stationery intended for typing and word processing, guides are included to facilitate the positioning of the type. Other guides indicate where the stationery should be folded to fit properly into the envelope. Envelope headings will give the name and address, leaving the telephone number to be included in the letter headings. The second page of stationery will be of the same design, but without the address and telephone number.

Letterheads are made for typewritten correspondence and appropriate stationery must be considered for handwritten correspondence. A4 letter size is recently most convenient for copying, and stationery corresponding to postal regulations is of considerable importance. But what should not be forgotten is the letterhead design's effectiveness and the reasons and purpose of the user. For an individual, the letterhead is merely for personal satisfaction, whereas for a company, an identity of the corporation must be realized with an understanding by the employees of the devised design.

Modern letterhead designs show boldness and variety, with images drawn over the entire surface of the stationery, usage in special types of paper, envelopes, writing paper and name cards that are coordinated, and stationery with front and back designs working in unison to convey a single idea.

On the whole, European stationery is relatively discreet in style, whereas in America where money is freely invested, the style is rather luxuriant. In Japan, generally they are not interesting or realistic, but remain, for the most part formal and subdued in feeling, perhaps because they are still looked upon by many companies as mere business supplies. There is no such concept in Japan as investing additional energy and expenses in this area.

But finer and more imaginative letterhead designs for typing and word processing are always being sought. In this era of office automation the letterhead design has re-established the value and relevance of the letter, in a sense opening our eyes once again to its message. The works collected in this book remind us in the same way of the living and thriving world of letterhead design.

Takenobu Igarashi

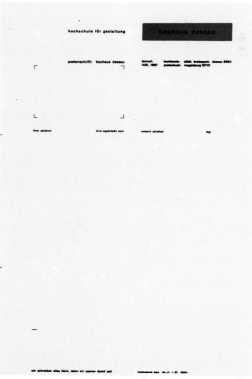

D/Herbert Bayer

はじめに

手紙を書くことは，人によって大変おっくうなことである。必要にせまられて書く場合など，大げさに言えば苦痛を伴うことさえある。その手紙も，受け取ることには悪い気がしない。それどころか親しい友人からのものや，遠い外国からのものなど，心ときめいて封を切るのももどかしいことさえ多い。手紙は，メッセージを積んだ紙の飛行船，といったようなロマンチックなイメージを抱かせる。

私信にしろ仕事上の手紙にしろ，手紙を受け取ると，そこに貼られている切手やその上に押されているスタンプ，受取人の住所氏名と差出人などをながめて，まず中身を推測するのが普通だろう。そのことによって，人は手紙の重要性を判断するのである。

また，手紙を書く方も，どのような便箋や封筒を使用するか，ペンで書くか筆なのか筆記具の選択から，切手の貼り方まで，個性や好みが目に見えるかたちで反映して，しかも残るから無神経ではいられない。

レターヘッド・デザインは，手紙のこのような性質や効果を上手に利用し，自分自身や会社を正確に相手に伝えようとするものである。

古くは，1925年頃より，ハーバート・バイヤーやジャン・チチョールドらによって，ヨーロッパで意欲的な実験が試みられている。活字や罫線を駆使したそれらの作品は，今みても感動を呼び起こすほど緊張感がみなぎっている美しい作品だと思う。これらのタイポグラフィカルな仕事は，主としてドイツやスイスのデザイナーに引き継がれ，やがて世界へと拡がったものと思われる。

レターヘッドとは本来，レターペーパーの頭部分に差出人の住所氏名を印刷したことから，手紙の頭にあるものという意味で使われ出した言葉だ。

レターヘッドのデザインも，当初は必要最小限の要素でデザインされることが多く(今日でも続いているが)，用紙やタイプフェイスの選定，住所氏名のレイアウトがその全てであった。積極的にデザイナーが参加し，大胆な発想が社会の中で取り入れられるようになったのは，高度成長期を迎えた1960年代のことである。それは長距離あるいは国際間のコミュニケーションが活発化し，郵便制度が発達し，タイプライターが普及したことと関係があるようだ。

特にアメリカでは，文房具店へ行けば個人でも簡単に専用の便箋，封筒，名刺が作れることから，この分野は急速に発達している。今日では，新しく事業を始めることは魅力的なレターヘッド・デザインを手にすることから始まる，とさえ言われるほどになった。

手紙は個人でも企業でも，その個性や主張を知らせる大切なメディアとして位置づけられている。言い換えれば，便箋や封筒によって我々が何者であるか，どこで仕事をし，どのような考え方を持っているのかを伝えることができる。また「強く個性的なデザインの封筒や便箋は，毎日届く多くの郵便物のなかで，その存在を際立たせ，部屋の遠くからでも見分けられる」と，アメリカのデザイナー，ロッド・ダイアーは語っている。

もう一人のデザイナー，ドン・ウェラーは，普通，便箋類はタイプされて使用されるが，「それは白紙の状態でも美しい」と，レターヘッド・デザインのそれ自体で完結する“美”についても指摘した。

手紙がタイプされる場合，その理由は“読み易く，短時間で，きれいに”といった合理的なものである。しかし，なかにはタイプの打ち方にも工夫して，個性的な手紙を書く人もいる。その極めつけの人物がアメリカのデザイナー，エイプリル・グレイマンだ。彼女は便箋を横にも斜めにもセットして，彼女の文章をレターヘッドのデザインの一部としてレイアウトする。大変な手間だと思うが，そのことによって，普通にタイプされた手紙にはない，人間性や考え方が伝わってくる特別な手紙になっている。これはレターヘッドのデザインの拡大解釈であり，新しい可能性を示す好例でもある。

楽しいあるいは相応しいレターヘッドデザインは，手紙を書く側にもその負担を和らげる効果をもた

らした。現在ではタイプライターやワードプロセッサーが普及して, 便箋に何らかの工夫が必要になってきたのも事実である。

そのデザインも最近は大胆になって, 便箋全体にイメージが描かれたものや, 特殊紙を使ったもの, 便箋, 封筒, 名刺が強い関連性を持ったもの, 表と裏がひとつのアイデアで連結するものなど, 多彩を極めている。

一般的に, ヨーロッパのものは比較的おとなしいデザインが多く, アメリカは自由でしかもお金をかけた贅沢なものが多い。日本は残念ながら面白いもの, 実験的なデザインが少なく, 保守的で類型的である。便箋, 封筒, 名刺にそれほどのエネルギーと費用を投入する発想がない。それらのものは会社では営業資材として位置づけられ, それ以上のメディア価値に目を向けない。

このようなレターヘッドのデザインにも, いくつかの基本がある。つまり, タイプライターやワープロ用であれば, 打出しの位置を示すガイドを活字の位置やデザインの要素で工夫するとか, 封筒に入れる場合の折り方のガイドを入れるとかである。表示内容についても封筒は住所氏名にとどめ, 便箋には電話番号も入れるとか, セカンドシートと言って, 手紙の2枚目からは, デザインは同じでも住所氏名の入らないものを用意する, などがそうだ。

用紙もタイプ向き, ペン書き用など, 筆記具の適正を考慮しなければならない。サイズにしても, 手紙の控え用に最近ではコピー用紙のA4サイズに等しくするのが便利だ。郵便料金の体系に見合った用紙の重量も考慮される。しかし, 何よりも重要なのは, 誰が何の目的で使うのか, そのデザインの効果に何を期待するかということだろう。個人用であれば, 使う人が満足すればよいかもしれない。会社のものであれば, 企業のアイデンティティを表示して, 社員の多くが納得するものを工夫しなければならない。

タイプライターやワープロ用であれば, 一層そこに何か心ときめく, すてきなアイデアやデザインが欲しい。レターヘッドのデザイン次第で, OA化時代の手紙の価値が変わるのである。そして既に, この本に収録された実例のように, レターヘッドのデザインの素晴しい世界が築かれているのである。

五十嵐威暢

jan tschichold ring nwg

absender: jan tschichold, münchen 23 ... 1 links

D/Jan Tschichold

Olle Eksell Sweden
Letterheads should be very individual. It makes no difference whether they are made for private use, for an association or a large industry. The letter is a means of private communication between two persons, between companies and individuals, associations and individuals, and therefore must be designed with 'intimacy', in a way that reflects the senders personality and distinct character. To meet today's standards of quality one needs a graphic designer with a highly developed sense of communication and the means to express it.

Michael Schwab United States
Letterheads are now so incredibly important. The concepts and designs are becoming so sophisticated. People now expect a strong statement from a letterhead. It is a very intense piece of business — a very creative piece of business.

F.H.K. Henrion England
When designing a letter paper - like any design job, it is important to be clear about objectives and the communication.

Designer's own letter paper
1 Does he wish to show his originality and uniqueness, his inventivness and capacity to innovate.
2 Does he wish to be seen as a professional consultant like a lawyer, an accountant or a surgeon: to be seen as competent, experienced, reliable, trustworthy and capable of dealing with any problem within his competence.
3 A combination of 1 and 2 as far as they are not mutually exclusive.
4 From the young designer or a newcomer to the field it is not possible to demonstrate experience or any of the attributes listed under 2. That these circumstances force him to solutions along 1.

General
A letterhead must always be seen as a total family of stationery: envelopes, business cards, compliment slips, lables etc. They must be seen as an open-ended system so that items can be added to the range as the need arises.
There is all the difference between a local photographer and a world-wide applicable stationery system. Like our designs for Coopers & Lybrand. In over 1000 offices in over 100 countries with widely varying legal requirements in each country and in different western, eastern and middle-eastern languages. Such a system, of course requires extensive research analysis and planning to arrive at an appropriate concept.

Les Mason Australia
The letterhead in business has become much like the suit and tie in business. Sometimes too safe. Maybe it makes it easy to borrow the necessary money but it doesn't do to show that a company is a progressive company. Let us hope that in the future the letterhead makes a more profound statement.

Giulio Cittato Italy
Good solutions are always personal. Letterheads work when the typographic structure does not interfere with the typewritten message. The letterhead design and the message have to live together in perfect harmony.

Tomoko Miho United States
Print outs from computer printers, word processors, et al, have increased the paper flow tremendously. Most sheets are imprinted with boring, 'gray' data. Good graphic design on stationery and business forms, reflecting a personality, is being introduced more and more. The creativity expressed is varied, colorful and often spirited.

Paul Davis United States
A letterhead always seems a simple project at first glance. But one quickly realizes that as an image that is dispersed to people all over the world, and often the only image they may see of an organization or individual, it must communicate a great deal. Creating the image is a complex task.
For many years I managed to get along without a letterhead by making a small drawing on each envelope. My first printed one was typeset by a printer in Sag Harbour. When I opened my studio in New York a few years ago, I finally designed the one you see. Now we're working on a new one. A single image isn't enough. I would like to change images with the seasons and not take it so seriously, perhaps returning to making a drawing on each envelope. I'd like to think of a letterhead as an ephemeral thing, like a leaf falling from a tree.

Fernando Medina Canada
Letterheads; putting one's best face forward.

Félix Beltrán México

The personal letterhead was created by the need to praise correspondence, which is now thriving. Paper is the medium through which the letterhead fulfills its objective in the world.
As the body of the letter is the focal point, the letterhead should lend support. Unfortunately, many letterheads only call attention through visual effects, often obscuring the individual's principal intent.

Pat Hansen United States

Letterheads, *when well designed*, function not only as a message carrying tool, but also as a display of a company's image. The image makes a statement about that company's product, services, attitudes, way of doing business, etc. The colors, typeface, and/or symbol are all working together in support of that image.
Some *common problems that we have noticed* in letterhead design include inappropriate use of colors, typeface, , and/or symbol design. If the design does not accurately make a statement about the company it represents, it is not successful.
Another common error is the tendency to ignore how the message or letter will appear in terms of logical alignment. The function of business stationery is to carry a message, therefore all pieces should have a balanced appearance that allows both image and message to have impact.
Problems we have personally experienced include clients that request something inappropriate or in the final stages changes the company's name, information to be included, or color. Also there have been occasions where there are too many decision makers within the company — 'design' by commmittee is difficult.

Rick Eiber United States

The letterhead designer is the modern shaman who creates visual magic to capture and maintain the attention of a disinterested, information overloaded public.
Every successful letterhead design enhances verbal communication in the same way a frame enhances a work of art.
A truly outstanding letterhead design extends beyond aesthetic harmony. It conveys positive messages about a sender's personality, status and business attitudes in a highly original form.

Heidi Rickabaugh United States

We feel that a letterhead, perhaps more even than a logo, sets the over-all image and tone for a company or an individual. A letterhead solution can come only from a total understanding of the client and his needs. The letterhead system is the most direct communication tool, setting the pace and form for all other printed materials as developed for a later time. In the case of the Seattle Art Museum, we utilized color to differentiate between various museum functions and departments, to give them their own identity within an umbrella system. It helped to organize the entire internal workings of the museum, while maintaining a consistent identity.

Barrie Tucker Australia

The design of a letterhead is often preceded by the creation and development of a symbol or logotype establishing the identity for a company, person or event etc. The letterhead is the most personalised presentation of the developed image and is an important instrument in projecting and promoting the imagery to the reciever. The letterhead design (incorporating a symbol, logo, typography and/or graphic forms and colour) must communicate the soul, character, a translation of the letterhead owner's philosophy, style and status.
The letterhead is not complete without typed matter (correspondence) added to it. The typing layout of the letter must be designed to complement the design of the letterhead.

Burton Kramer Canada

Our letterhead designs are almost always a basic part of a visual identity program we develop for a given client. Most often we will have designed a symbol or logotype, a use of type style and other graphic elements and the use of color, to convey a distinctive personality. Our stationery designs are developed to look best in conjunction with a typed letter, an address and stamp on the envelope, an address on a label and with a typed, complete invoice or business form. All elements are designed to function in cooperation with the material for which they are intended, and are never designed to be 'just a pretty face'. The particular flavour of each solution will reflect the nature, style and quality of each organization, product or service.

Olle Eksell Sweden

レターヘッドは，大いに個性的であるべきだと思います。個人用のものでも，団体用また大企業用のものでも，同様のことがいえます。手紙というものは，個人同士，会社と個人，また団体と個人の間のプライベートなコミュニケーション手段です。ですから，手紙の送り手の個性や特徴を伝える"親密感"のあるデザインにする必要があります。今日的な価値基準に見合うだけの，コミュニケーションに対する高度のセンスとそれを表現できるグラフィックデザイナーが要求されるわけです。

Michael Schwab United States

レターヘッドは，極めて重要な存在になってきています。コンセプトもデザインも，たいへん高度なものになりつつあります。人々は，レターヘッドから明確なメッセージを期待しています。それは，強力なビジネスの一部品，非常に創造的なビジネスの一部品なのです。

F.H.K. Henrion England

レターペーパーをデザインするときには，デザインの他の分野と同様，目的とその伝達方法の明確化が重要です。
デザイナー自身のためのレターペーパー——
(1)自分の独創性，創意工夫の能力，新規なものを取り入れる能力があることを示したいのか……。
(2)自分が弁護士，会計士または外科医のようなプロのコンサルタントであると見られたい，即ち有能で経験があり，信頼に応えることができ，自分の適性範囲でいかなる問題も処理できる力があることを示したいのか……。
(3)互いに矛盾しない限り(1)と(2)の両方を示したいはずです。
(4)若いデザイナーやこの分野に入りたての人には，経験やその他(2)に列記された事柄を実証することは不可能です。そこで，(1)の線に沿った方法を探るしかありません。
一般用——
レターヘッドは，常にトータルなステーショナリー類，即ち封筒，名刺，礼状，ラベルなどのうちのひとつとして考慮されなければなりません。必要に応じて別の要素を足していけるように，幅広い利用が想定されている必要があります。
また，例えば一写真家のレターヘッドと，世界的に使用されるステーショナリーとでは，大きな違いがあるものです。私たちがデザインしたクーパー＆ライブランドの場合，100以上の国に1,000以上のオフィスがあり，各国で異なった法律規制があるうえ，使用言語も西洋，東洋，中東に分かれています。このような場合，適切なコンセプトに到達するには，広範な調査分析とプランニングが必要であることはいうまでもありません。

Les Mason Australia

業務用レターヘッドは，ビジネス・スーツやネクタイと同じような感覚で受けとめられるようになっています。そこで，時に，当たりさわりのないものになりがちです。その方が経費として要求しやすいのかも知れませんが，反面,その会社が進歩的な会社であることが反映されないことにもなりかねません。今後は，レターヘッドがもっと強烈な自己表現をするようなものになることを願いたいものです。

Giulio Cittato Italy

良いデザインは，常に個人的なものです。レターヘッドは，印刷部分とタイプされた書簡文とがうまく融け合っているときに初めて成功とみなされます。レターヘッドのデザインとメッセージは，完全に調和して共存するものでなければなりません。

Tomoko Miho United States

コンピュータ・プリンター，ワードプロセッサーなどによる印刷物は紙の氾濫に大いに拍車をかけました。ほとんどの紙には退屈な"没個性"のデータが刷り込まれています。しかし，その一方で，書簡用紙や事務用紙に個性を反映させた好ましいグラフィックデザインも次々と紹介されています。表現された創造性は千差万別で，色彩感に溢れ，活気に満ちたものがしばしば見られます。

Paul Davis United States

レターヘッドの仕事は，最初はいつも簡単に思えます。しかしそれは，世界中の人々に送られ，その個人なり会社なりの最初のイメージを伝えるものであって，そこには豊かなコミュニケーションの力が備わっていなければいけない，ということに気づかされます。そうしたイメージの創造は，かなり複雑な作業といえるでしょう。
長年の間，私は封筒に一つひとつ小さな絵を描いて，レターヘッドなしですませてきました。最初に印刷した私の作品は，陰鬱なハーバーの町の印刷屋に活字組みしてもらったものです。数年前ニューヨークにスタジオを開いたとき，やっとデザインしたのが，ここに掲げたレターヘッドです。今は新しいレターヘッドのデザインに着手しています。一つのイメージだけでは不充分です。季節ごとに図柄を変え，あまり固く考えないようにしています。もしかしたら以前の，封筒ごとに絵を描く方法に逆戻りしているかも知れません。
私はレターヘッドを，木から落ちる葉のような移ろい行くものとしてとらえたいのです。

Félix Beltrán México

個人用レターヘッドは，通信文を賞揚する必要からつくられたもので，現在大流行しています。用紙はレターヘッドが世間に出てその目的を達成するための媒体，ということになります。

最も大事なのは手紙の本文であり，レターヘッドはそれを補助するものでなければなりません。残念ながらレターヘッドの多くはその視覚的効果に意を注ぐばかりで，当人の主要意図をあいまいにさせていることがままあります。

Fernando Medina Canada

レターヘッド。自分の一番いい顔を見せること。

Pat Hansen United States

レターヘッドは，うまくデザインしてあるときには，単にメッセージを伝える道具としてだけでなく，企業のイメージを表現する媒体として機能します。そのイメージから企業の商品，サービス，姿勢，営業方針などをつかむことができます。刷り色，タイプフェイス，シンボルといった要素が一つに溶けあって，企業のイメージを支えるのです。

レターヘッドのデザインでよく見かける基本的な間違いのひとつに，こうした刷り色，タイプフェイス，シンボルの選択ミスという問題があります。デザインが企業の性格を正確に映し出していないものでしたら，それは明らかに失敗作といえるでしょう。

メッセージや手紙の文章がどのような配列で並ぶのかという問題を無視するということも，よくありがちな失敗例です。事務用のステーショナリーの機能は，まずメッセージを伝えるという点にありますから，すべての要素がバランスよく配置されて，イメージとメッセージをともに強調するようでないと，良いデザインとはいえないでしょう。

私たちが個人的に抱えている問題のひとつは，クライアントにあります。理屈にあわないことを要求したり，間際になって社名などの情報や色を変更したいと言い出したりするのです。一社の中に決定権を持つ人間が多すぎるときもありました。"デザイン"を複数の人間で考えようとするのは無理な話です。

Rick Eiber United States

レターヘッドのデザイナーは，無関心で情報過多な人々の注意をもひきつける力を持った視覚的魔術を行なう，現代のシャーマンです。成功したレターヘッドのデザインは，例外なく言葉によるコミュニケーションのわくを拡げるようなものばかりです。額縁が絵画をよりひきたてるのと同じ効果があるのです。

Barrie Tucker Australia

レターヘッドのデザインに先立って，企業や個人，あるいはイベントのアイデンティティを確立するためのシンボルやロゴタイプが創り出され，展開されるのはそう珍しいことではありません。というのは，レターヘッドはそのようにして展開されたイメージの，最も私的なプレゼンテーションであり，手紙を受けとる側にイメージを投影して，自分の言いたいことをアピールするための重要な手段だからです。シンボル，ロゴ，タイポグラフィ，グラフィックのフォルムや色などで構成されるレターヘッドのデザインは，感情や性格，あるいは使い手の哲学，スタイル，地位までも伝えるものでなくてはなりません。

Heidi Rickabaugh United States

レターヘッドは，企業や個人のトータル・イメージやトーンをロゴ以上に雄弁に語ります。どういう要素をもりこむかは，クライアントをトータルに認識し，相手がどんなことを望んでいるかを知ることによって決まります。

レターヘッドというのは最も直接的なコミュニケーション手段ですから，後になって他の印刷物をつくるときにも参考になるでしょう。シアトル・アート・ミュージアムの場合は，美術館の機能や部署別に色分けし，ひとつの包括的な機構のなかでのそれぞれのアイデンティティという意味あいを表現しました。こうすることで，各セクション固有の特色を保ちながらも，美術館の内部作業全体を系統づけるのに役立っています。

Burton Kramer Canada

私たちのレターヘッドは，クライアントのために開発するヴィジュアル・アイデンティティ・プログラムのなかでも，基本的な分野となっています。シンボルやロゴタイプをデザインし，タイプフェイスやグラフィック，配色などを決定し，クライアントの個性を引き出そうとしています。私たちがデザインするステーショナリーは，タイプされた文字をのせたレターヘッド，宛名書きをして切手を貼った封筒，住所を打ったラベル，タイプしたインヴォイスやビジネスフォームというように，用途が完成した時点でいちばん美しく見えるようにつくられています。すべてのデザイン要素は使用目的に沿うように配慮されており，ただ"きれいだから"という理由で無意味に付け加えられているものはひとつもありません。つまり，そうしたデザイン・ソリューションの一つひとつは，各企業，製品，サービスの性質やスタイル，あるいは品質を反映するために採用されているのです。

Nancy Epstein Gallery
Gallery
画廊
USA 1986
Dyer/Khan Inc.
AD/Rod Dyer
D, A/Paul Morgan

Better Made in Britain
Helping British Industry
イギリス製品振興事業
England 1985
Michael Peters + Partners
AD/Glenn Tutssel
D/Glenn Tutssel, Alison Cane

PRESS INFORMATION

BETTER
MADE IN
BRITAIN
From Sir Basil Feldman
Chairman of the Exhibition

BETTER
MADE IN
BRITAIN
From Sir Basil Feldman
Chairman of the Exhibition

With compliments
39/40 St James's Place
London SW1A 1NS
Telephone 01 493 3178/9

39/40 St James's Place
London SW1A 1NS
Telephone 01 493 3178/9

Square One
Restaurant
レストラン
USA 1984
Gerald Reis & Company
AD, D, A/Gerald Reis

SQUARE ONE

SQUARE ONE

THE RESTAURANT AT
GOLDEN GATEWAY COMMONS
190 PACIFIC AT FRONT
SAN FRANCISCO 94111

SQUARE ONE

THE RESTAURANT AT
GOLDEN GATEWAY COMMONS
190 PACIFIC AT FRONT
SAN FRANCISCO 94111
TELEPHONE 415 788-1110

THE RESTAURANT AT
GOLDEN GATEWAY COMMONS
190 PACIFIC AT FRONT
SAN FRANCISCO 94111
TELEPHONE 415 788-1110

SF/A
Retail Clothing & Housewares Store
衣料品・家庭用品店
USA 1983
Gerald Reis & Company
AD, D, A/Gerald Reis

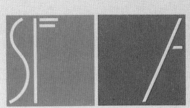

130 WEST PALACE
SANTA FE
NEW MEXICO
87501
505 982 5212

3500 CENTRAL AVE. S.E.
ALBUQUERQUE
NEW MEXICO
87106
505 266 2222

130 WEST PALACE
SANTA FE
NEW MEXICO
87501

Jim Myers
Photographer
写真家
USA 1986
Krause & Young Inc.
AD/Bob Young

JIM MYERS • PHOTOGRAPHER
165 COLE • DALLAS, TEXAS 75207
TELEPHONE • 214 • 698 • 0500

JIM MYERS • PHOTOGRAPHER
165 COLE • DALLAS, TEXAS 75207

JIM MYERS • PHOTOGRAPHER
165 COLE • DALLAS, TEXAS 75207
TELEPHONE 214 • 698 • 0500

LAURA THOMAS

Jacqui Morgan
Illustrator
イラストレーター
USA 1985
Gonda Design, Inc.
AD, D/Tomás Gonda
A/Jacqui Morgan

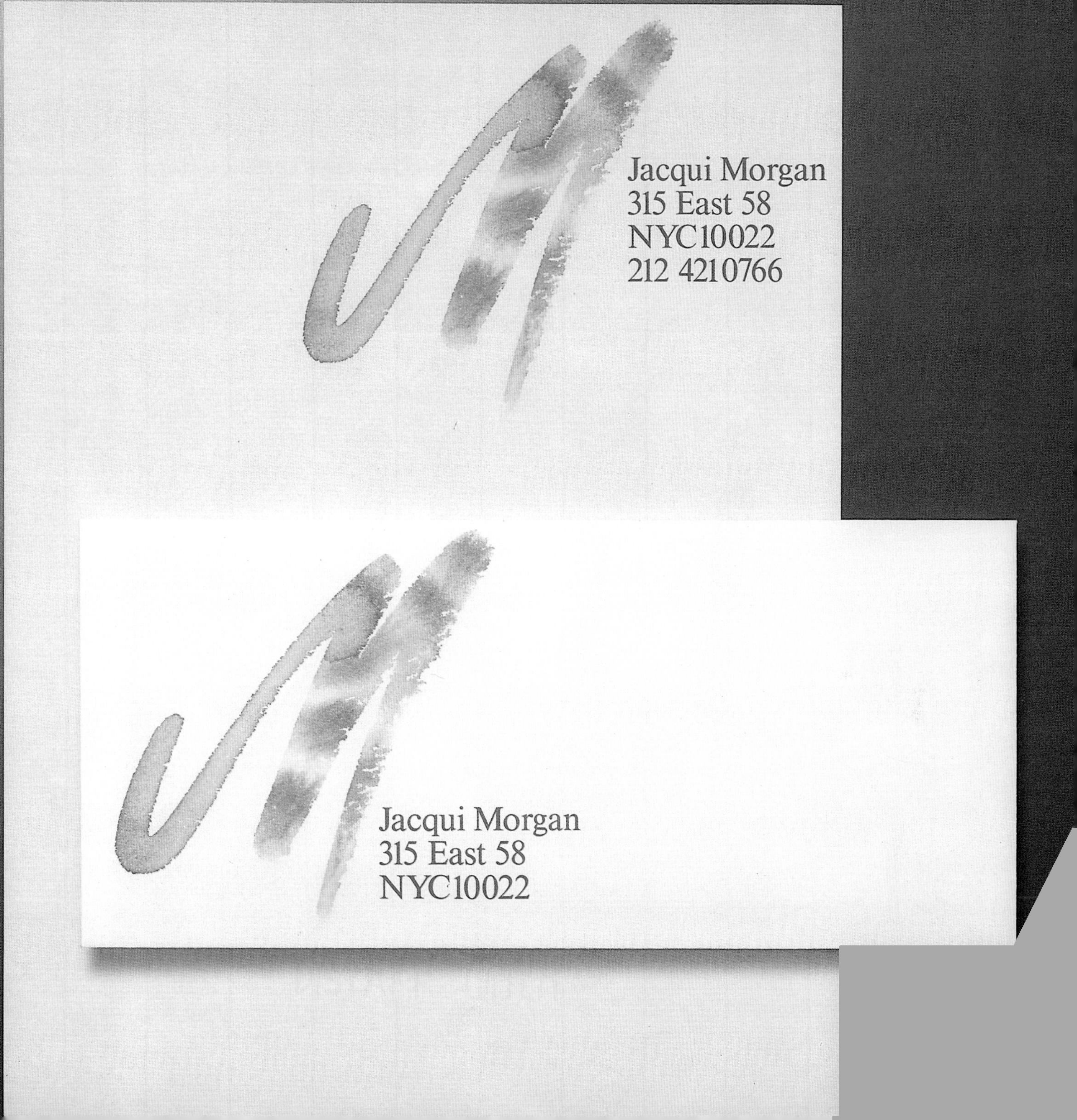

Jacqui Morgan
315 East 58
NYC10022
212 4210766

Jacqui Morgan
315 East 58
NYC10022

Myrna Davis
Graphic Designer
グラフィックデザイン
USA 1984
Paul Davis Studio
AD/Paul Davis
D/Paul Davis, José Conde

Myrna Davis
14 East 4th Street
New York, NY 10012
212 674·5708

Myrna Davis
14 East 4th Street
New York, NY 10012
212 674·5708

Myrna Davis
14 East 4th Street
New York, NY 10012

Karen Rapp Interiors
Interior Design
インテリアデザイン
USA 1986
La Pine/O'Very Inc.
AD, D, A/Julia La Pine, Traci O'Very Covey

KAREN RAPP INTERIORS

KAREN RAPP INTERIORS

5207 NORTH 24TH STREET
SUITE 108
PHOENIX, ARIZONA 85016

5207 NORTH 24TH STREET
SUITE 108
PHOENIX, ARIZONA 85016
602-956-3575

Karen Rapp Interiors
Interior Design
インテリアデザイン
USA 1986
La Pine/O'Very Inc.
AD, D, A/Julia La Pine, Traci O'Very Covey

Foothill Design Group
Architecture
Landscape Architecture
Planning
Environmental Analysis
408 J Street
Marysville, CA 95901
916.742.2426

Foothill Design Group
Architecture
Landscape Architecture
Planning
Environmental Analysis
408 J Street
Marysville, CA 95901

Foothill Design Group
Architecture
Landscape Architecture
Planning
Environmental Analysis
408 J Street
Marysville, CA 95901
916.742.2426

Lynn S. Pomeroy
Principal

Oregon Rainbow Inc.
Publishing
出版
USA 1976
Rickabaugh Design
AD/Robin Rickabaugh, Heidi Rickabaugh
D/Robin Rickabaugh

MusiCum Laude
Writing & Production of Movie Music
映画音楽の著作・製作
USA 1986
The Weller Institute
for the Cure of Design, Inc.
AD, D/Don Weller
A/Chikako Weller

Campbell & Scott
Advertising Consultancy
広告コンサルタント
USA 1985
Les Mason Graphic Design
AD,D/Les Mason
A/Lino Giangiordano

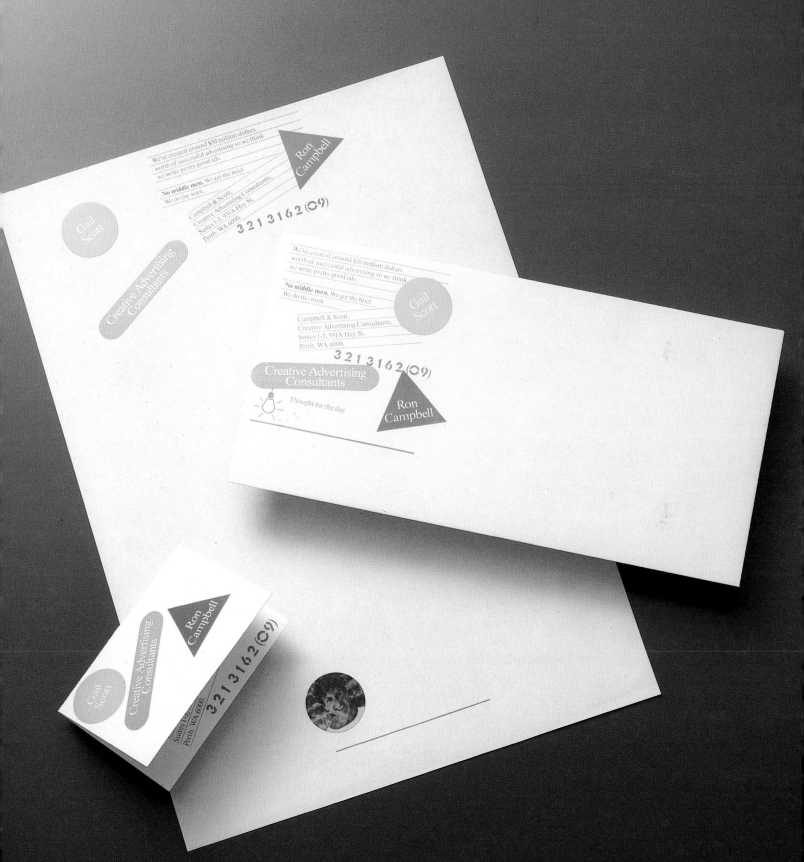

Robert Mondavi &
Baron Philippe de Rothschild
Production of Premium Wines
高級ワイン製造
USA 1984
Pate International
D/Susan Roache Pate, Hock Wah Yeo

P.O. BOX 6
OAKVILLE
CALIFORNIA 94562
707 963 1979

P.O. BOX 6
OAKVILLE
CALIFORNIA 94562

ROBERT MONDAVI · BARON PHILIPPE DE ROTHSCHILD

H. STUART HARRISON JR
PROJECT MANAGER

P.O. BOX 6. OAKVILLE
CALIFORNIA 94562
707 963 1979
415 433 1979

ROBERT MONDAVI · BARON PHILIPPE DE ROTHSCHILD

Darby Graphics
Printing/Communications
印刷会社
USA
James Leinhart Design
D/James Leinhart

28 29

DARBY GRAPHICS, INC. 4015 N. ROCKWELL STREET CHICAGO, ILLINOIS 60618 PHONE 312-583-5090

DARBY GRAPHICS, INC.   4015 NORTH ROCKWELL STREET CHICAGO, ILLINOIS 60618 312-583-5090

DENNIS FRANTSVE

DARBY GRAPHICS, INC.
4015 NORTH ROCKWELL STREET
CHICAGO, 60618 PHONE 312-583-5090

Brenda French
Fashion
ファッション
USA 1986
Tomoko Miho Co.
AD, D/Tomoko Miho

BRENDA FRENCH

BRENDA FRENCH

3860 Centinela Ave. Los Angeles, California 90066

Showroom: 110 East 9 St. Suite C839
Los Angeles, California 90079
213 624 9272

Showroom: 485 Seventh Ave. Suite 404
New York, New York 10018
212 971 0110

Corporate Offices: 3860 Centinela Ave.
Los Angeles, California 90066
213 313 1833 Telex: 295301

Lettergraphics SA Pty Ltd.
Designer and Manufacturer of
Architectural Signage
建築標識のデザインと製作
Australia 1985
Barrie Tucker Design Pty Ltd.
AD, D/Barrie Tucker
A/Mark Janetzki

Dona Emerson
Seamstress
女性裁縫士
USA 1982
Harry Murphy + Friends
AD, D/Harry Murphy

Dona Emerson
Seamstress

622 Northern Avenue
Mill Valley, Ca. 94941

Telephone
415 383-2551

Dona Emerson
Seamstress

622 Northern Avenue
Mill Valley, Ca. 94941

Dona Emerson
Seamstress

622 Northern Avenue
Mill Valley, Ca. 94941

Telephone
415 383-2551

Jack Milan
Nouvelle Cuisine Catering
料理ケイタリング
USA 1981
Laughlin/Winkler
AD, D/Mark Laughlin, Ellen Winkler

d i f f e r e n t   **tastes** . . . .

178 west brookline street
boston/massachusetts 0 2 1 1 8

catering and consulting

617 536 2416

jack milan

d i f f e r e n t
tastes

617 536 2416

catering and consulting

Katrin Adam & Associates
Architecture
建築
USA 1985
Works
AD/Katrin Adam
D, A/Keith Godard

Barrie Rokeach Aerial Photography
航空写真
USA 1982
Michael Patrick Cronan Design, Inc.
AD,D/Michael Patrick Cronan

34　35

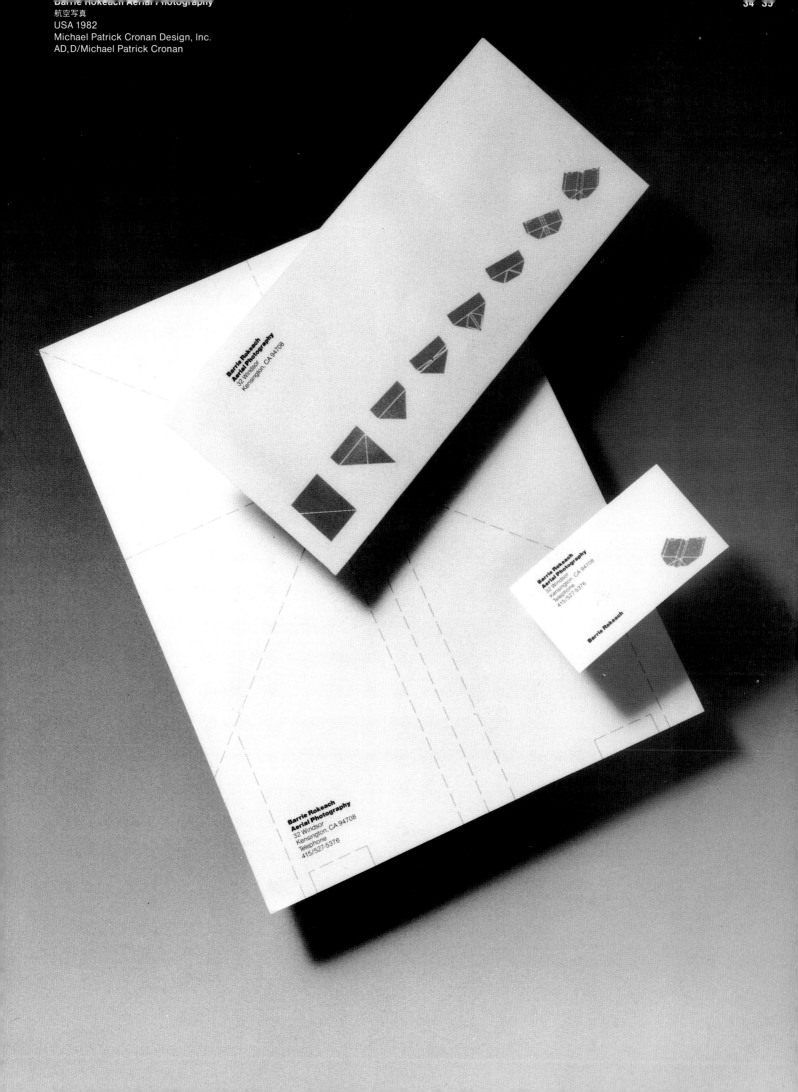

Tokiwa Printing Co., Ltd.
Printing Company
印刷会社
Japan 1983
Igarashi Studio
AD/Takenobu Igarashi
D/Hiromi Nakata

Laser Ten Inc.
Lighting Company
照明会社
Japan 1983
Igarashi Studio
AD/Takenobu Igarashi
D/Hiromi Nakata

Guy Rolland
Photographer
写真家
USA 1985
Richardson or Richardson
AD,D/Forrest & Valerie Richardson

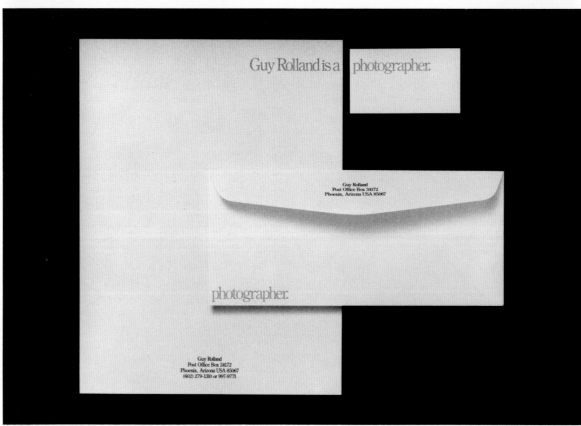

The Rand Corporation
Research Firm
調査会社
USA 1986
Sussman/Prejza & Co.
AD/Deborah Sussman
D/Gigi McGee, Corky Retson

Cervia Ambiente
Ecological Association
生態学協会
Italy 1979
Giulio Cittato
AD, D/Giulio Cittato

Operahouse Zürich
Theater
劇場
Switzerland 1986
AD, D/Domenig Geissbühler

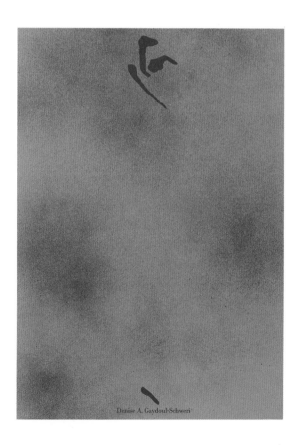

Jo Langmoen
Lumber Dealer
林木商
Switzerland 1984
AD, D, A/Domenig Geissbühler

Denise Gaydoul
Personal Letterhead
個人用レターヘッド
Switzerland 1985
AD, D/Domenig Geissbühler
A/Guillaume Borel

Alberto Orio
Kitchen Furniture
台所用家具
Italy 1982
Giulio Cittato
AD, D/Giulio Cittato

Susana Klik
Designer
デザイナー
Spain-Austria 1984
Medina Design
AD, D, A/Fernando Medina

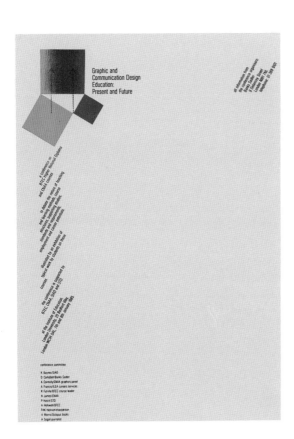

Design Education Conference
デザイン教育協議会
England 1986
AD, D, A/F.H.K. Henrion

Andy Jllien Shoes
ファッション・シューズ
Switzerland/USA 1978
2D3D
AD, D, A/Jonathan Louie

Ink on Paper
Art prints Organization
美術印刷協会
Netherlands 1985
D/Pieter Brattinga

Jay Freis
Photography
写真
USA 1983
Michael Schwab Design
AD, D, A/Michael Schwab

ink·on paper

Lauriergracht 80, 1016 RM Amsterdam, tel. 020-241491

JAY FREIS

PHOTOGRAPHY

416 RICHARDSON / SAUSALITO, CA 94965 / USA / 415-332-6709

KvK Amsterdam 174830   Postgiro 5553878, Amro Bank 44.57.41.007 Amsterdam

S·J Engineering Inc
32 Gifford Street
Toronto, Ontario
M5A 3J1
Telephone:
(416) 960-0778

guadalupe velázquez diseño gráfico cto. economistas d-22 cd. satélite edo. de méxico cp. 53 100 tel. 5 62 67 48

S & J Engineering Inc.
Engineering
エンジニアリング
Canada 1982
Burton Kramer Assoc. Ltd.
AD/Burton Kramer
D/Karl Martin, Burton Kramer

Guadalupe Velázquez
Graphic Design
グラフィックデザイン
México 1984
Félix Beltrán & Asociados
D/Guadalupe Velázquez, Félix Beltrán
A/Guadalupe Velázquez

Art gallery, Fine Furniture Sales
画廊・高級家具販売
México 1986
AD, D, A/Maria Theresa Echartea

Gary Braasch
Photographer
写真家
USA 1980
Rickabaugh Design
AD/Robin & Heidi Rickabaugh
D/Robin Rickabaugh

42 43

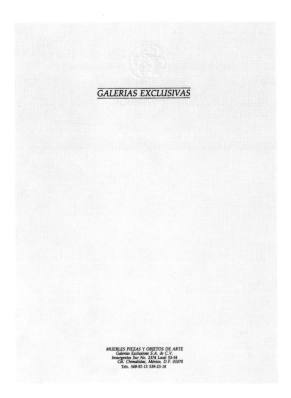

Frida Szniger
Graphic Design
グラフィックデザイン
México 1984
Félix Beltrán & Asociados
D/Frida Szniger, Félix Beltrán
A/Frida Szniger

Norman Diekman
Interior and Furniture Design
インテリア・家具デザイン
USA 1985
George Tscherny, Inc.
AD, D, A/George Tscherny

Jean Myers Architectural Glass
Architectural Glass Artist
建築用ガラスデザイン
USA 1979
Pentagram Design
D/Kit Hinrichs

JEAN MYERS ARCHITECTURAL GLASS
POST OFFICE BOX AG • SOUTH LAKE TAHOE • CALIFORNIA • 95705 • PHONE (916) 541-7878

Jean Myers Architectural Glass
Architectural Glass Artist
建築用ガラスデザイン
USA 1979
Pentagram Design
D/Kit Hinrichs

Corzo & von Kalinowski
Industrial Design
インダストリアルデザイン
USA 1982
Wayne Hunt Design, Inc.
AD/Wayne Hunt
D/Norma O'Neill

Corzo & von Kalinowski

1245 Roslyn Lane
La Jolla, California 92037
619·454·9939

Corzo & von Kalinowski

**The International Review of
Food & Wine**
食品・ワイン雑誌
USA 1978
The Pushpin Group
AD/Jessica Weber
D/Alan Peckolick
A/Tony DiSpigna

William Helburn
Photography and Film Production
写真および映画製作
USA 1979
Gene Federico
AD, D/Gene Federico

46 47

HELBURN.

William Helburn Productions, Inc.
352 Park Avenue South NY 10010
(212) 683-4980

Pierre Janssen
Art Critic
美術評論家
Netherlands 1986
D/Pieter Brattinga

Pierre L.A. Janssen
Noordereind 10
4012 BT Kerk-Avezaath
tel. 03448-1768

TEN
Cable TV
有線テレビ
England 1985
Michael Peters + Partners
D/Maddy Bennet

48 49

THE ENTERTAINMENT NETWORK
SEVENTH FLOOR
48 LEICESTER SQUARE
LONDON WC2H 7LZ

TELEPHONE 01-930 7810
TELEX 948928 TENLDN-G

A DIVISION OF UNITED CABLE PROGRAMMES LTD
REGISTERED NUMBER 1747019 ENGLAND
REGISTERED OFFICE 48 LEICESTER SQUARE LONDON WC2

ICOGRADA
Design Seminar
デザイン・セミナー
England 1985
AD, D, A/F.H.K. Henrion

in Collision with Tomorrow
11th Icograda Student Seminar
11/12 February 1985 Odeon Cinema
Leicester Square London
Chairman: FHK Henrion

Information from
the organisers:
Banks Sadler
9 Delancey Street
London NW1 7NL
Tel: 01-388 9101

Gallery MA
Gallery of Interior Architectural Design
画廊
Japan 1985
Ikko Tanaka Design Studio
AD/Ikko Tanaka
D/Ikko Tanaka, Kan Akita
C/TOTO Co., Ltd.

TOTO NOGIZAKA BLDG, 3F 1-24-3 MINAMI AOYAMA, MINATO-KU,
TOKYO JAPAN TELEPHONE(03)402-1010 TELEX 2223581 TOTOTY J

Embrey Press Inc.
Fine Printing
印刷
USA
AD,D/Glen Iwasaki

Rick Levine
Film Director
映画監督
USA 1986
Lou Dorfsman, Inc.
AD/Lou Dorfsman
A/Jim Shefcik

Rick Levine Productions, 59 East 82nd Street, New York, New York 10028 (212) 734-9600 / 9026 Melrose Avenue, Los Angeles, California 90069 (213) 271-8506

City Golf
Indoor Golfing
屋内ゴルフ
W. Germany 1985
Mendell & Oberer
AD, D/Pierre Mendell

The Finger Print Company
Publishing Company
出版社
Australia 1980
Barrie Tucker Design Pty Ltd.
AD, D/Barrie Tucker
A/Robert Marshall

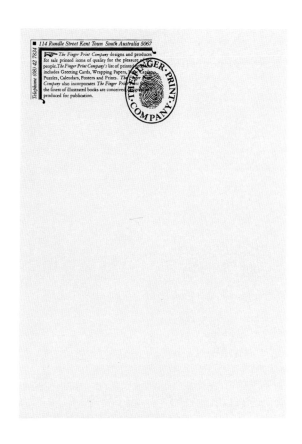

Gráfica Magazine
Art Publication
美術出版
Brazil 1984
Miran Studio
AD, D/Oswaldo Miranda

Evans Preschool Daycare Center
保育所
USA 1983
Bottoni Design
AD, D/Joseph Bottoni

Videotex-Forum
Information Service
情報サービス業
Switzerland 1985
Gottschalk + Ash International
D/Fritz Gottschalk, Frederic Burbach

Monty & Myrtle Berman
Personal Letterhead
個人用レターヘッド
England 1981
Pentagram Design
D/Mervyn Kurlansky, Paul Vickers

videotex

Myrtle Berman
2 Hillside
Highgate Road
London NW5 1QT
01-485 7482

Videotex-Forum
Birkenstr. 21
8306 Brüttisellen
Telefon 01/833 33 11
Telex 52 862

PIED A TERRE

Marcia
Wertheimer

Pied à Terre
1159 Third Avenue
New York New York
10021

212
570
0550

olsky
322E39ST
NY10016
MU6-2597

M
Soko

Pied a Terre
Shoe Boutique
シューズ・ブティック
USA
Plumb Design Group Inc.
D/Kathleen Bordelon, Susan Ritzau

Melvin Sokolsky
Photography and Film Production
写真および映画製作
USA 1959
Gene Federico
AD,D/Gene Federico

BPCC Video Graphics
Computer Graphics and Animation
コンピュータ・グラフィックおよびアニメーション
England 1986
Quay & Gray
D/David Quay
A/Paul Gray

Bauhaus
.Art and Techniques Magazine
美術技法雑誌
Italy 1985
Rinaldo Cutini
D/Rinaldo Cutini

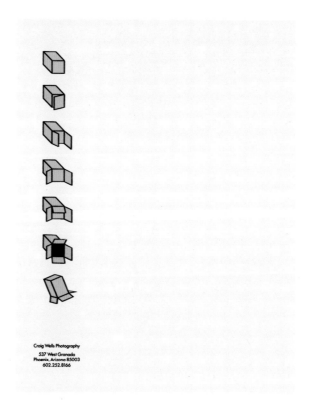

Ebert, Hannum, & Volz
Architects
建築家
USA 1983
Vanderbyl Design
AD, D, A/Michael Vanderbyl

Craig Wells Photography
Corporate Photographer
写真家
USA 1985
Richardson or Richardson
AD, D/Forrest & Valerie Richardson

HBR Display Industries Pty Ltd.
Industrial Design
インダストリアルデザイン
Australia
Ken Cato Design Company
AD, D/Ken Cato

Connectives Inc.
Communications Consultancy
コミュニケーション・コンサルタント
USA 1979
McCoy & McCoy
AD, D/Katherine McCoy

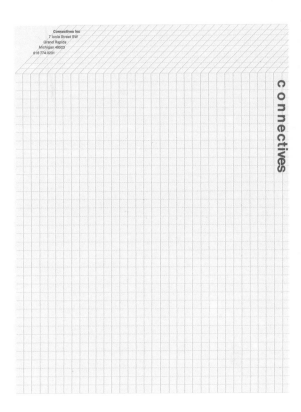

Rodeo Collection
Galleria
画廊
USA 1978
Saul Bass/Herb Yager & Associates
D/Saul Bass, Art Goodman
C/Pacific Triangle Development Corp.

Fernando Medina
Designer
デザイナー
Canada 1982
Medina Design
AD, D, A/Fernando Medina

ORIX Corporation
Consulting Company
コンサルティング会社
USA 1985
Igarashi Studio
AD/Takenobu Igarashi
D/Debi Shimamoto

David Bellman Gallery
Art Gallery
画廊
Canada 1981
Gottschalk + Ash International
AD/Stuart Ash
D/Nita Wallace

ORIX
CORPORATION

134 Pear Street
D A V I D
Third Floor
B E L L M A N
Toronto, Canada
G A L L E R Y
M5V 2H2

416 / 363-2308

The Galleria
117 East 57 Street
New York NY 10022
Tel: 212-752-4133
Telex : 427434 SMNY

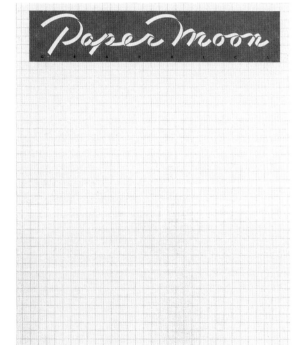

P.O. Box 34672 · Los Angeles, Ca. 90034 · (213) 659-9053 · Telex: 181867 PAPERMOON CULV

CHARLES
COURY
VINEYARDS
503-357-7802
DAVID HILL ROAD
PO BOX NO 372
FOREST GROVE
OREGON
97116

Papermoon Graphics
Illustration
イラストレーション
USA 1982
Mike Fink Graphic Design
AD/Linda Barton
D, A/Mike Fink

Charles Coury Vineyards
Winery
ワイン製造業
USA 1977
Rickabaugh Design
AD/Robin & Heidi Rickabaugh
D/Heidi Rickabaugh

**California Council for
the Humanities**
カリフォルニア人文科学会議
USA 1982
Sussman/Prejza & Co.
AD/Deborah Sussman
D/Debra Valencia

The Forum Collection, Inc.
Furniture & Interiors
家具・インテリアデザイン
USA 1985
Sussman/Prejza & Co.
AD/Deborah Sussman, Debra Valencia
D/Stephan Silvestri
A/Felice Mataré

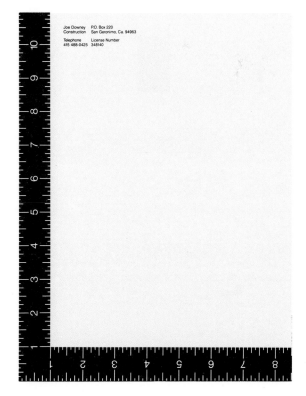

The Steve Tisch Co.
Film Production
映画製作
USA 1986
Dyer/Kahn, Inc.
AD/Rod Dyer
D, A/Paul Morgan

Joe Downey
Construction
建設
USA 1981
Harry Murphy + Friends
AD, D/Harry Murphy

ACM Siggraph '86
Computer Graphics Convention
コンピュータ・グラフィック大会
USA 1985
Pirtle Design
AD/Woody Pirtle, Luis Acevedo
D, A/Luis Acevedo

Sealander & Company
Copywriting
コピーライティング
USA 1979
AD/Woody Pirtle, Rex Peteet
D, A/Rex Peteet

ACM SIGGRAPH 86   13th Annual Conference
on Computer Graphics and
Interactive Techniques
Dallas, Texas
August 18-22

Conference Management
Smith, Bucklin and Associates, Inc.
111 East Wacker Drive
Chicago, IL 60601 USA
312 644 6610
Telex 25 4073 SBA

Co-Chairs
Ellen Gore
Raymond L. Elliott

Sealander & Company
2711 Wood, Unit H
Dallas, Texas 75219
(214) 522-0144

Mead World Headquarters, Courthouse Plaza N.E., Dayton, Ohio 45463

Arnold Harwell McClain & Associates, Inc.
Advertising-Marketing-Public Relations
3434 Fairmount, Dallas, Texas 75219 (214) 521 8400

The Mead Paper Company
紙会社
USA 1985
Pirtle Design
AD/Woody Pirtle
D/Woody Pirtle, Jeff Weithman
A/Jeff Weithman

Arnold Harwell McClain & Associates
Advertising Agency
広告代理業
USA 1981
Pirtle Design
AD/Woody Pirtle
D, A/Frank Nichols

Renaissance Remodeling
Building & Remodeling
建築・改築業
USA 1978
Gerald Reis & Company
AD, D, A/Gerald Reis

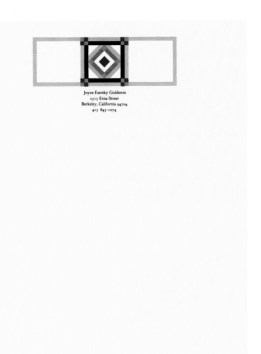

Charles Kemper Photography
写真
USA 1985
Michael Patrick Cronan Design, Inc.
AD/Michael Patrick Cronan
D/Michael Patrick Cronan, Nancy Paynter

Dean Follis
Photographer
写真家
USA 1983
John Follis & Associates
AD/John Follis
D/Jean Claude Muller

Paper & Ink
Paper Specialities Shop
紙製品販売店
USA 1978
The Pushpin Group
AD, D/Alan Peckolick

WM de Majo England
... To find solutions which are different and original, yet practical, especially from the user's point of view and when the design needs to conform to stringent and often very mundane postal regulations.
... Problems arise often also when one needs to use a window envelope which requires a deeper and sometimes wasteful heading or when creating a matching design for an envelope and when the most useful position can usually not be used because printing would have to be done across 2 or 3 layers of paper (other than in cases of very large runs where envelopes can be printed in the flat, unfolded state).
Many of the most exciting layouts, especially/in letterhead design competitions are not so practical when text has been typed on to the heading or much space is wasted along the top and which is normally not acceptable to a commercial client who wants to get as much text as is reasonable onto the heading.

Skolos, Wedell & Raynor United States
When designing a letterhead we try to create an environment that will enhance a communication. The written message and its setting (the letterhead) complement each other and play off of each other rather symbolically.

George Tscherny United States
There are basically two directions in letterhead design. One is to simply identify the sender, the other is to go beyond fulfilling this minimum requirement by becoming an advertisement for the sender as well.
Both the Air Canada and Norman Diekman letterheads belong to the second category.
The strong repeat pattern on the backside of the Air Canada logo identifies the sender even before the letter is unfolded. However, once it is unfolded, the design does not intrude on the reader or on the written message.
Instead of repeating the identical design on all items for Norman Diekman's stationery, the letterhead, envelope and business card were each given a different treatment, yet with a common vocabulary which gave them all a family resemblance.
The torn paper shape on the letterhead is intended to approximate the yellow tissue paper on which architects and interior designers sketch, and Mr. Diekman's distinctive signature was reproduced on the business card.

Rolf Harder Canada
Even in this age of electronic communication, the letterhead still has an important function. Tangible and personal, it is a document that is, at times, the sender's sole representative.
I see the designer's task as creating stationery that is pleasing to the eye, eloquent in expressing the sender's personality, readily identified and last, but not least, easy and practical to use.

Tomás Gonda United States
Letterheads, like trademarks, more often than not are loaded with the responsibility of being the sole bearers of the company image.
Letterheads may well be the first phase of an introduction but they should be part only of a larger, comprehensive graphic program.
I do letterheads only, only for friends.

Forrest Richardson United States
Richardson or Richardson approaches letterhead design in much the same way we approach other design projects. That approach involves identifying the problem, formulating a goal, and then developing solutions that will help make the goal a reality. In this method the end result should speak to everything we defined in the beginning: what does the client need, what can the client afford, who will be using the end product, etc.
Since most of our stationery projects are only a small part of the work we are contracted to do for a client, we tend to pattern letterhead assignments after overall identities. Everything is taken into consideration; signage needs, interiors, advertising, brochures, etc. In short, a well designed letterhead is only as good as the other design system a client has. For instance, a poorly put together marketing package can easily overshadow a great letterhead. A mailing label that was an afterthought can spoil a fine letterhead.

Heinz Waibl Italy
A person's or Company's letterhead is by far the most important document in printed visual communication. Free creativity finds little scope in a letterhead and in this light a letterhead may become itself a creativity test. The role of the computer can be a useful one in developing the basic creative idea once this has been found.

Katherine McCoy United States

First of all, a letterhead must always be designed with the letter that will be typed or handwritten on it in mind. The composition of the letterhead should position and organize the letter. The design should guide the typist to type in the correct position. That is why I dislike centered letterhead compositions — they might look good without a letter on them, but they ignore the fact that western letters are typed with a flush left margin.

Secondly, a letterhead must interpret the nature of the client and the characteristics of their work. The design should reflect their personality accurately, with a sense of joy and anticipation for what the letter will say. A letterhead is only as interesting as the person for which it is designed.

Kurt Wirth Switzerland

Concerning letterhead for our personal use, it is natural that we expect a great deal from ourselves. In the business-world letterhead that is both suitable and beautiful is rare.

The computer age has brought many restrictions to our creative freedoms. It has brought not only advantages, but also disadvantages. Taking over old or unsightly logos is another problem we face. When the structure of a company is very complicated, and all the divisions, subdivisions and branch production teams are present, then the letterhead becomes a description of the company. And when the entire management board throws its two cents in on the design/creation, we have a problem. Difficulties abound.

Ellen Winkler United States

During all our years of designing letterheads, 'identities', we have found that the most interesting and stimulating pieces have been designed for new businesses.

We work hand in hand with the client in trying to establish their image. Each is unique, as in the case of 'Ralph Mercer Photography', where he wanted his letterhead to do 'all the talking'. He wanted a 'new wave' look — his image was a primary concern because he didn't like to write.

For all the new business clients we stress the importance of a credible identity right in the beginning. As soon as they open the doors to a new business — ie 'You can run your business out a locker at a bus station as long as you LOOK credible on your letterhead, and it accurately communicates what you do'.

Weisz & Yang United States

Letterhead and stationery systems are unique design problems. The physical restrictions and parameters rarely change, ie, size, format, envelope shape, etc.; these are fairly standard. However, the visual problems change for each new client or job. Whether it be a corporation or a personality, the letterheads must be expressive of that identity. The letterhead must be clear and precise in its expression and also not interfere with the presentation of the primary information, ie, the letter.

Yarom Vardimon Israel

The president of a large Israeli industry interrupted my presentation as I was trying to explain the concept for their new stationery. 'Letters?' he said. 'Our business is mainly conducted through telex and telephone; wouldn't it be worth our while to invest in a new visual scheme under such circumstances?' The answer had to be YES.

A letterhead is a good communication vehicle where design qualities can support anything from personal needs to marketing requirements.

Letterheads should be used for inside corporation purposes only — one should still design them — in a way that will support corporation pride, mutual respect and a personal feeling of belonging.

M. Zender United States

Letterheads are one of the few 'incomplete' things designed by a graphic designer — incomplete in the sense that it is never used as designed — but always has a significant design element added to it by a non-design person — a *secretary*.

This makes for an interesting collaboration between designer and user in the production of the end product!

To be accurately judged, a letterhead should be viewed with a letter typed on it. A letterhead without a letter is truly a non-functional thing.

Also interesting is the communication role of the letterhead. Graphic designers are constantly involved in communication — by nature so are letterheads! Ironic that so many letterhead designs ignore the main communication element, the written letter.

PDC 2
Design Showrooms
デザイン・ショールーム
USA 1982
April Greiman Inc.
AD, D, A/April Greiman

PDC 2
Members

Arc-Com Fabrics, Inc.
Artemide
Atelier International, Ltd.
Beelner & Thomas
Ben Rose, Inc.
Brickel Associates Inc.
Design Tex Fabrics West
Executive Office Concepts
Forms + Surfaces
The "G" Showroom

The Gunlocke Company
Haller Systems
Harbor Universal | Benadetti Corp.
Harbor Corporation
Harter Corporation
Hauserman
Haworth
Herman Miller Inc.
ICF Inc./Unika-Vaev U.S.A.
Kasparians, Inc.
Kimball and Artec
Knoll International
Krueger
Pacific-Condi Focus
Ron Rezek/Lighting
Scandiline/CADO
The Shaw-Walker Company
Shelby Williams Industries
Stendig | B & B America
Stow/Davis Furniture Company
Sunar
Westinghouse Open Office System

P D C 2

Contract
Manufacturers
Association
West Coast

PDC 2
Pacific Design Center
Second Floor ±270
8687 Melrose
Los Angeles
California 90069

Contract
Manufacturers
Association
West Coast

PDC 2 **Pacific Design Center**

Vertigo
Clothing & Accessories
衣類・アクセサリー・ブティック
USA 1979
April Greiman Inc.
AD, D, A/April Greiman

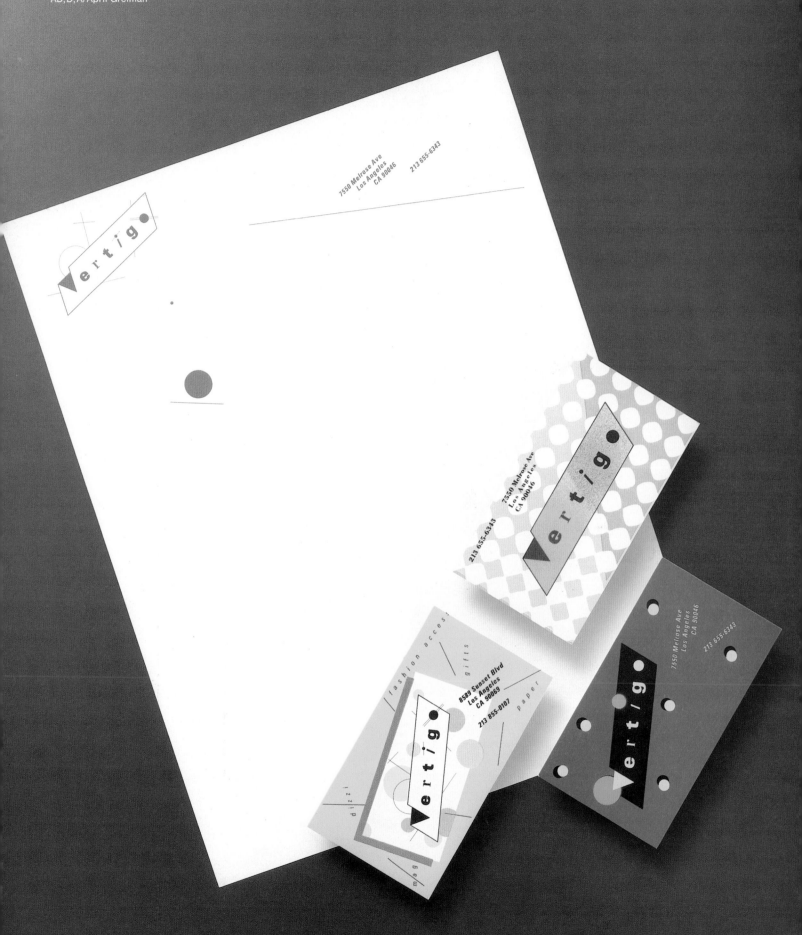

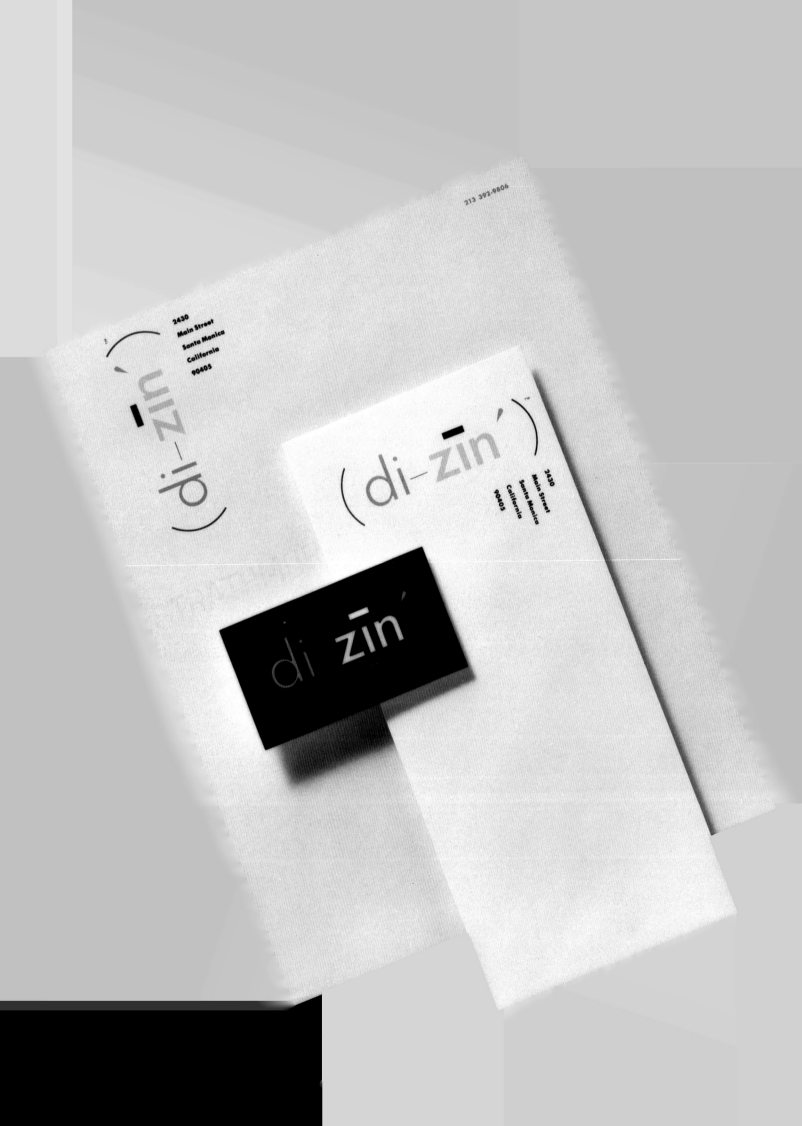

Calypso

485
S. Robertson
Suite 1
Beverly Hills
California
90211

Landscape Design
Planting
Maintenance

213   2 7 3 - 8 6 6 0

Calypso

485
S. Robertson
Suite 1
Beverly Hills
California
90211

Landscape Design
Planting
Maintenance

Interior

Calypso

485
S. Robertson
Suite 1
Beverly Hills
California
90211

Landscape Design
Planting
Maintenance

213   2 7 3 - 8 6 6 0

Swid Powell
Architect and Tableware Designer
建築・食器デザイン
USA 1985
Skolos, Wedell & Raynor
D/Nancy Skolos

LYCEUM

Fellowship

LYCEUM

Fellowship

1000 Massachusetts Avenue   Cambridge, Massachusetts 02138

1000 Massachusetts Avenue   Cambridge, Massachusetts 02138

(6 1 7) 5 4 7 - 5 4 0 0

Pamela Bruce Associates
Corporate Interior Design
企業インテリアデザイン
USA 1985
Skolos, Raynor & Wedell
D/Cheryl Lilley

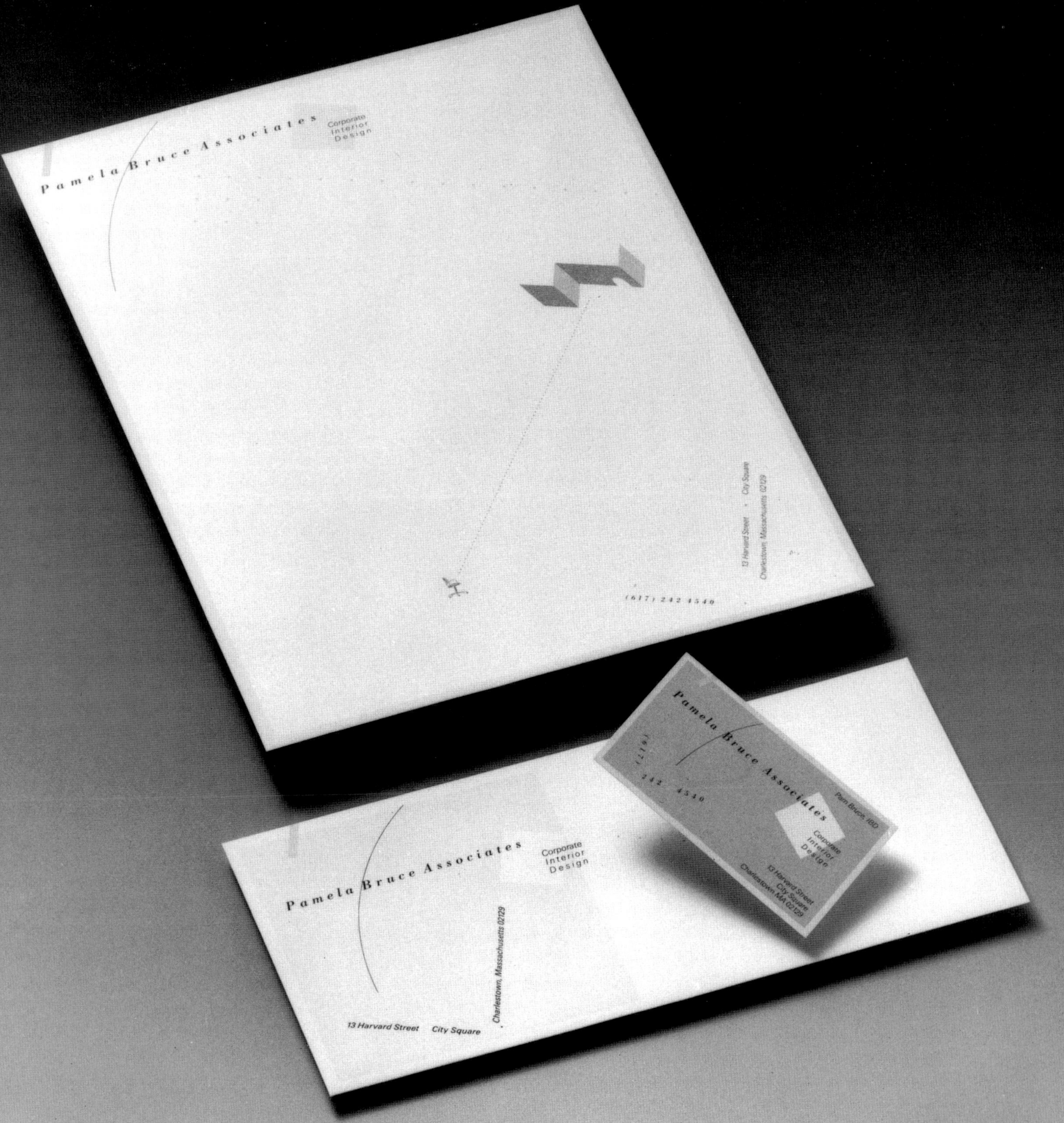

Todd & Kathy Schorr
Illustration
イラストレーション
USA 1985
Mike Fink Graphic Design
AD, D/Mike Fink

Interprint
Printing
印刷
USA 1982
Michael Patrick Cronan Design, Inc.
AD, D/Michael Patrick Cronan

72 73

Gindick Productions Ltd.
A video, film and slide show
production company
ビデオ・映画・スライド製作
USA 1985
Pentagram Design
AD/Colin Forbes
D/Maryann Levesque

Jim Evanson
Architecture and Sculpture
建築・彫刻
USA 1984
Weisz & Yang Inc.
D/Larry Yang, Doug Banquer
A/Jim Evanson

Cincinnati Composer's Guild
シンシナティ作曲家組合
USA 1985
Zender & Associates
AD/Mike Zender
D/Priscilla Fisher

Faith Evangelical Free Church
福音教会
USA 1986
Zender & Associates
AD/Priscilla Fisher
D/Mike Zender

76 77

Bannerworks, Inc.
Banner Design and Production
旗のデザイン・製作
USA 1985
Pat Hansen Design
AD, D/Pat Hansen
A/Pat Hansen, Al Doggett

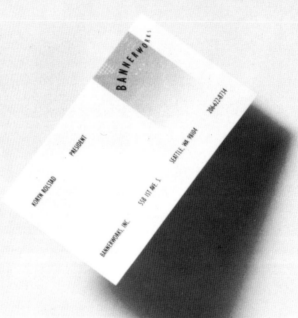

BANNERWORKS, INC.   558 1ST AVE. S.   SEATTLE, WA 98104   206-622-8734

Al Costello
Film Production
映画製作
Switzerland 1985
Bruno Monguzzi
AD,D/Bruno Monguzzi

Stimulus
Video Production Company
ビデオ製作
USA 1984
Bunny Zaruba Graphic Design
AD,D/Bunny Zaruba
A/Grant Johnson

STIMULUS

P.O. ■ Box ■ 11621
San Francisco
C A ■ USA ■ 94101
415 558-8339

Fausto Gerevini
Photography
写真
Switzerland 1983
Oberholzer Tagli Cevio
AD,D/Sabina Oberholzer, Renato Tagli

80 8

Fausto Gerevini   fotografo   via Borghese 12
CH-6600 Locarno
093 31 47 57

Locarno

Fausto Gerevini   fotografo   vi invita il 5 giugno
dalle 18.00 alle 20.00   presso dillo, casa Magoria,
via Panigari 5, Locarno

espone dal 5 al 28 giugno 1985

Fausto Gerevini   fotografo   via Borghese 12
CH-6600 Locarno
093 31 47 57

Deutscher Designertag/EV
Association of German Graphic,
Industrial and Photographic Designers
ドイツのデザイン協会
W. Germany 1977
BK Wiese Visual Design
AD, D/BK Wiese

Kammer Jazz Ensemble Kiel
Jazz Band
ジャズバンド
W. Germany 1985
BK Wiese Visual Design
AD,D/BK Wiese

The Type Gallery, Inc.
Typography
タイポグラフィー
USA 1985
Rick Eiber Design
AD,D/Rick Eiber

Ralph Mercer
Photographer
写真家
USA 1984
Laughlin/Winkler
AD,D/Mark Laughlin, Ellen Winkler

84 85

r a l p h
mercer
photography

369 w union st
e bridgewater/MA
02333

617   378 7512

Interiors Plus
Interior Decorating
インテリア
USA 1985
Laughlin/Winkler
AD, D/Mark Laughlin, Ellen Winkler

Thoresen & Associates
Mental and Physical Health Care
健康管理業
USA 1985
Laughlin/Winkler
AD, D/Mark Laughlin, Ellen Winkler

Interiors Plus, Inc

316 Central Street
Saugus/MA 01906

617   233 0550

Interiors Plus
Interior Decorating
インテリア
USA 1985
Laughlin/Winkler
AD, D/Mark Laughlin, Ellen Winkler

Thoresen & Associates
Mental and Physical Health Care
健康管理業
USA 1985
Laughlin/Winkler
AD,D/Mark Laughlin, Ellen Winkler

Bindas Studios
Photography
写真
USA 1981
Laughlin/Winkler
AD, D/Mark Laughlin, Ellen Winkler

86 87

Thoresen and Associates

T

1891 Professional Building
Suite 215
Liberty Square
Danvers/MA 01923

617 774 0011

Bindas Studios 205 A street Boston MA 0 2 2 1 0
617 2 6 8 / 3 0 5 0

Intomart Qualitatief
Market Research
市場調査
Netherlands 1982
TD Associates
D/Daphne Duijvelshoff-van Peski

Intomart Qualitatief

achterom 152,
1211 pd hilversum nederland
telefoon 035, 16355* telex 43921
postgiro 4459228
n.m.b. rek.nr. 67.56.12.373

uw referentie

onze referentie

hilversum,

hr. gooiland 33048

lid abg-groep

CLB
Central Laboratory of the Dutch
Red Cross Blood Transfusion Service
オランダ赤十字輸血サービス中央研究所
Netheriands 1986
TD Associates
D/Reynoud Homan,
Daphne Duijvelshoff-van Peski

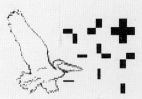

amsterdam —

central
laboratory
of the
netherlands red cross
blood transfusion
service

plesmanlaan 125
1066 CX amsterdam
PO box 9190
1006 AD amsterdam
telephone 020 512 9222

department —

direct telephone number —

reference —

your reference —

cable SANGUIS
telex 13159 BLOOD NL
bankers
amrobank 43 78 30 470

Felderman + Associates Inc.
Architecture
建築
USA 1983
April Greiman Inc.
AD, D, A/April Greiman

KGO-TV
Television Company
テレビ会社
USA 1985
Bunny Zaruba Graphic Design
AD/Bunny Zaruba, Jim Stringer
D, A/Bunny Zaruba

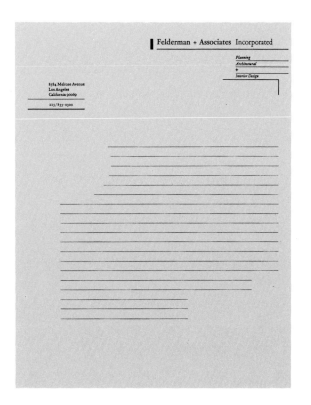

J.D. Looseleaf
Fabrication of Vinyl Binders
ビニール・バインダー製造
Canada 1984
Burton Kramer Assoc. Ltd.
D/Burton Kramer, Debbie Adams

Doyle Graf Mabley
Advertising
広告業
USA 1986
Fred Troller Associates
AD, D/Fred Troller

Küng Blockflötenban
Recorder Manufacturer
録音機メーカー
Switzerland 1983
Odermatt & Tissi
AD, D, A/Rosemarie Tissi

Arche Verlag
Editing
出版編集
Switzerland 1983
Odermatt & Tissi
AD, D, A/Rosemarie Tissi

90 91

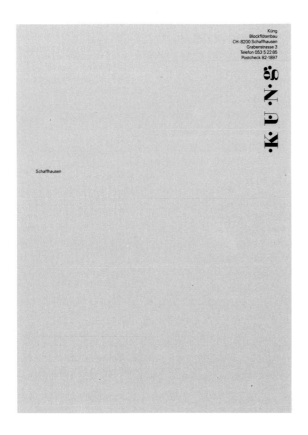

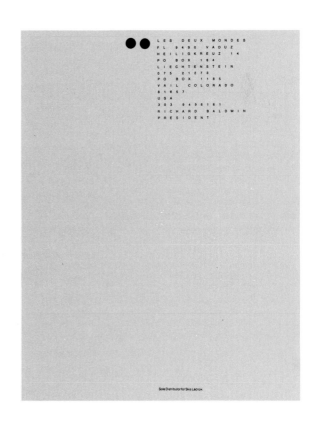

Lucida Communications
Marketing Company
マーケティング会社
Australia 1986
Emery Vincent Associates
AD, D/Garry Emery

Les Deux Mondes
International Winter Sports
Equipment Distributor
冬季スポーツ用具販売
USA & Liechtenstein 1980
Rudolph de Harak & Assoc.
D, A/Rudolph de Harak

WM de Majo England

レターヘッドのデザインで大切なのは，他とちがうオリジナリティと実用性を持ち，使う人の立場に立っていて，厳格で妥協の余地のない郵便法の規則にも合致しているようなデザイン・ソリューションを見つけることです。

その際問題になるのは，次のような状況にぶつかったときです。たとえば窓つき封筒をつくるとなると，レターヘッドのヘッディング，つまり見出しを下に下げるなり，まったく無駄なヘッディングを付けたりしなくてはなりません。また，封筒と便せんを同じデザインにすると，封筒の紙の重なりがじゃまをして，封筒のヘッディングの重要なパートがかすれてしまったりします。封筒の印刷部数が大量の場合は，製袋する前のフラットな紙の状態で印刷できますので，こういうことは起こりません。

特にデザイン・コンペに出品されるようなレターヘッドは，レイアウトが非常にすぐれていますが，ヘッディングに合わせてテキストをタイプしてみると，意外に使いにくかったりするものです。

Wiesz & Yang United States

レターヘッドやステーショナリーには，デザインの上で独特の問題があります。物理的な制約もさることながら，パラメーター，すなわちサイズ，フォーマット，封筒の形などが変わることはめったにありません。どれもだいたい標準が決まっています。ただし，ヴィジュアルな問題に関しては，新しいクライアント，新しい仕事に関わるたびに変わります。レターヘッドは明解かつ正確な表現力を持ち，主たる情報，すなわち手紙の判読を妨げないデザインでなければならないのです。

Kurt Wirth Switzerland

プライベートに使うレターヘッドをつくるときには，あれもこれも取り入れたいと思うのは当然だと思います。業務用の場合は，用途に沿っていてなお美しいデザインというのには，まずお目にかかれません。コンピュータ時代はデザイナーの創作上の自由にさまざまな制約をもたらしました。長所があれば欠点もあります。古いロゴ，みっともないロゴをリデザインするのが，私たちの当面の課題です。

企業の機構が非常に複雑で，部，課，下請けなど枝分かれしている場合には，レターヘッドがその企業の説明になります。経営陣がデザインやクリエイティブなことにあれこれ口を出しすぎるのも問題です。

本当に難しい問題がたくさんあります。

Skolos, Wedell & Raynor United States

レターヘッドをデザインする際には，コミュニケーションをさらに深めるための環境づくりを心がけています。タイプされた通信文とその背景（レターヘッド）は相互に補い合い，やや象徴的な意味で競い合うかたちになります。

Tomás Gonda United States

商標と同じように，レターヘッドはその会社のイメージの唯一の担い手としての責任を負わされることが多々あります。レターヘッドが，個人や会社の紹介の第一歩であるのはもちろんですが，同時により大きな，総合的なグラフィック・プログラムの一部でなければなりません。

私は，レターヘッドをデザインするのは友人のためだけに限っています。

Forrest Richardson United States

レターヘッド・デザインに対する私たちの取り組み方は，他のデザイン・プロジェクトに対する取り組み方と何ら変わるところはありません。まず問題点を見つけ出し，目標を定め，そして目標を現実化するのに役立つ方法を探っていきます。そして，その結果として，最初にめざしたすべてのこと，即ちクライアントが何を求めているか，クライアントの許容範囲，誰がその完成した作品を使用するのか，というようなことに対する解答になっていなければなりません。

私たちのステーショナリー・プロジェクトは，ほとんどの場合，契約に基づいてクライアントのために行なっている仕事の一部に過ぎませんから，全体のアイデンティに従ってレターヘッドを作成します。そこでは，サイン，インテリア，広告，パンフレットといったすべてのことが考慮されるのです。要するにすぐれたレターヘッド・デザインもクライアントが有する他のデザイン・システムと変るところはありません。例えば，統一性のないパッケージ・デザインは，最高のレターヘッドをも台無しにし，後からの思いつきによるメール用ラベルも素晴しいレターヘッドを無意味なものにしてしまいます。

Heinz Waibl Italy

個人，あるいは企業のレターヘッドは，印刷媒体のヴィジュアル・コミュニケーションの手段として，最も重要な役割を果たすものです。自由な創造力を発揮するには制約がありますので，レターヘッドをデザインするということは，逆にデザイナーの創造性をためす機会であるともいえるでしょう。一度，ベースとなる概念を確立すれば，コンピュータの諸機能も，その概念を応用していくのに便利なものとなります。

Rolf Harder Canada

このエレクトロニック・コミュニケーションの時代においても，
レターヘッドは依然重要な役割を持っています。形のある
パーソナルな書類として，送り手の人となりを代表する唯一
の手段にもなり得ることがあります。
目に快く，送り手の個性をいきいきと表現し，一目見てその
人のものだとわかるようなレターヘッドをつくるのがデザイナ
ーの役目だと私は思います。最終的には，むろん"最低で
も"という意味ではありませんが，使いやすい実用的なデザ
インにしなくてはならない，というのが私の考えです。

Katherine McCoy United States

まず最初に，レターヘッドはその上にタイプされる，あるいは
手書きで書かれる文章があることを，常に頭においてデザ
インしなくてはなりません。レターヘッドのレイアウトは手紙の
文章を正しい位置におき，その形を整える働きをする必要
があります。タイピストが正しいポジションから手紙を打ち
始めることができるデザインにするべきなのです。
ですから私は，センターぞろえのレターヘッドが好きになれま
せん。文章がタイプされる前の見た目はきれいですが，欧
米人の手紙は常に左ぞろえで打つという事実を無視してい
るからです。
第二に，レターヘッドのデザインはクライアントの性質と仕
事の内容を伝えるものでなくてはなりません。クライアントの
性格を正確に伝えると同時に，何が書いてあるのだろうと
いう期待を感じさせるようなデザインが望ましいと思います。
どういう人が使うかによって，レターヘッドの面白味もちがっ
てきます。

Ellen Winkler United States

長年レターヘッド，つまり"アイデンティティ"をデザインして
きましたが，いちばん面白かったのは，新しく設立された企
業のためのデザインにたずさわったときです。
私たちはクライアントと協力して，その会社のイメージを確
立しようとしてきました。どれもユニークなものばかりでした
が，特に"ラルフ・マーサー・フォトグラフィ"の場合は，彼が
レターヘッドにすべてを語らせようとした点で新しいものでし
た。ニューウェーブ風のデザインを，ということでした。文章
を書くのが好きではなかった彼にとっては，イメージを伝える
というのが最大の関心事だったのです。
新しく事業を発足させたクライアントに対しては，信頼される
アイデンティティを最初から確立する必要性を強調しまし
た。新事業の開始とともに「レターヘッドが，あなたの会社
の信頼度を表現し，業務内容を正確に伝えるデザインに
なっていれば，バス停においたロッカーでも商売ができま
す」と言うのです。

Yarom Vardimon Israel

私が，イスラエルのある大手企業のために開発する新しい
ステーショナリーのコンセプトを説明しようとしたとき，社長
が私のプレゼンテーションをさえぎって，「手紙だって？　う
ちの会社はテレックスと電話で商売してるんだ。今さら新し
いヴィジュアル化計画に投資する必要があるのかね?」と
言うのでした。
答えはイエスでなければなりません。
レターヘッドはすぐれたコミュニケーションの手段であり，デ
ザインの質さえよければ，個人の需要からマーケティングま
でどんな用途にも対応できます。
レターヘッドはその企業の社内目的にのみ使われるべきも
のですが，企業としてのプライド，互いの信頼，帰属感と
いった感情を支えるようなやり方で，各人がさらに工夫をこ
らしていくのが大事だと思います。

George Tscherny United States

レターヘッドのデザインにはふたつの方向性があります。ひ
とつは送る側のキャラクターをシンプルに表現するもの，い
まひとつはそうした最低条件をふまえたうえで，さらに送る側
の宣伝材料となることをめざそうとするもの。

M. Zender United States

レターヘッドは，グラフィックデザイナーが手がけるデザイ
ンのなかでも数少ない"未完成"の作品です。未完成という
意味は，デザインされた状態のままで使われる場合は皆無
で，その上に必ず際立ったデザイン要素が，デザインとは
無関係の人間，つまり秘書によって付け加えられるからで
す。
こうしてデザイナーとユーザーの間で，完結した作品を使っ
て再び制作に入るという，興味深い共同作業が行なわれま
す。
正確にいえばレターヘッドは，文字がタイプされた状態で
見た方がよいのです。文章の書かれていないレターヘッド
など，無意味なのですから。
もうひとつ興味深いのは，レターヘッドの通信面での役割
です。グラフィックデザイナーは常にコミュニケーションと関
わっているわけですが，これこそまさにレターヘッドの本来の
性質なのです。皮肉なことに，多くのレターヘッドのデザイ
ンが，コミュニケーションという主要な機能，つまり手紙を書
くという状態を無視してつくられていますが……。

Nava/Divisione Porsche Design
Porsche Design Distribution in Italy
イタリア・ポルシェブランドの販売
Italy 1981
Unidesign
AD, D/Walter Ballmer

Olivetti Controllo Numerico spa
Office Machines
事務機器
Italy 1982
Unidesign
AD, D/Walter Ballmer

94 95

Capitale sociale lire 2 miliardi
CCIA Ivrea 322473
Casella Postale 2/19117
Reg. Soc. Tribunale Ivrea n. 994

10090 S. Bernardo d'Ivrea (Torino)
Telefono (0125) 64500
Telex 50041
Telegrammi: Meccanica Olivetti Ivrea

Olivetti Controllo Numerico spa

Distinta spedizione n.　　Data

Conferma ordine n.　　Data

Consegna

Resa

Mezzo

Imballo

Codice	U.M.	Quantità richiesta	Quantità spedita	Descrizione

Matricola　　Tensione　　Frequenza

Annulla e sostituisce　　Data

Istruzioni particolari:

Nota consegna　　Data　　Fattura

Centro emittente　　Centro utente e comme

Marcatura colli　　Peso netto　　Peso lordo

Quantità colli　　Numerazione colli

Spedizione a mezzo

Consegna da produzione　　Data　　Visto

Firma corriere　　Data di compilazione O

Ufficio gestione prodotto

Capitale sociale lire 2 miliardi
CCIA Ivrea 322473
Casella Postale 2/19117
Reg. Soc. Tribunale Ivrea n. 994

10090 S. Bernardo d'Ivrea (Torino)
Telefono (0125) 64500
Telex 50041
Telegrammi: Meccanica Olivetti Ivrea

Olivetti Controllo Numerico spa

ns. rif.　　vs. rif.　　data

olivetti
OCN

10090 S. Bernardo d'Ivrea (Torino)

olivetti
OCN

sildamin®

Sildamin spa
alimenti e sistemi
per la zootecnia

27010 Sostegno di Spessa
Pavia
Telefono 0382.79176 (5 linee)
Telex 321107 Sildam I

CC Postale 12963278
Codice Fiscale e Partita IVA
00176680189

data   prot. n.

---

fattura

sildamin®

Sildamin spa
alimenti e sistemi
per la zootecnia

27010 Sostegno di Spessa
Pavia
Telefono 0382.79176 (5 linee)
Telex 321107 Sildam I

CC Postale 12963278
Codice Fiscale e Partita IVA
00176680189

Capitale sociale 4.000.000.000
interamente versato

CCIAA Pavia 23354
iscrizione registro società
Tribunale di Pavia n. 951
fascicolo 1811

agente	cliente	condizioni di pagamento		data	numero	data	numero
				bolla di consegna		fattura	

cod. prod.	descrizione della merce		u.m.	quantità	prezzo unitario	sconto pag.	prezzo netto	importo

imponibile iva

iva

aliquota iva

ni 089

(*) 0 mangime semplice. 1.3.
composto integrato. 2.4.6.
mangime composto integrat
8 integratore. 9 apparecchiat

Condizioni di vendita. La me
di porto. Dopo 8 giorni dall'av
senz'altro accettata. Il pagan
sede legale della venditrice.
venditrice e non comportare il
al termine stabilito per il paga
sua esclusiva scelta, sospen
il contratto senza dover alcun
ro di Pavia. La merce è stata f
dichiarazioni e indicazioni pr

ni 088

---

settore suini
servizio genetica

sildamin®

Sildamin spa
alimenti e sistemi
per la zootecnia

27010 Sostegno di Spessa
Pavia
Telefono 0382.79176 (5 linee)
Telex 321107 Sildam I

			scrofa															genealogia				
tipo scheda	codice organizz.	all.	razza		numero			tatuaggio				linea genetica						genitori	razza	numero	tatuaggio	linea gen.
1 2 3	4 5 6	7	8 9	10	11 12	13 14 15	16 17 18											padre				
2 2 0																		madre				

verro   numero   tatuaggio linea gen.   data copertura

presunta parto

marcare

nati vivi/anno   **svezz.**/anno   **parti**/anno

tipo scheda	numero parto	data parto			nati morti	mumm.	nati vivi		peso in kg.		U N F	anorm. MC E	numero progress. covata		parto vuoto	codice svezz.
		giorno	mese	anno			maschi	femmine								
19	20 21	22 23	24 25	26 27	28 29	30 31	32 33	34 35	36 37	38 39	40 41	42 43 44 45 46	47 48 49 50 51 52 53 54 55 56	80
0														

tipo scheda	numero parto	data perdita			cause perdita								data perdita			cause perdita								codice svezz.
		giorno	mese	anno	S	KK	PI	AA	MM A	GD	COLI	DIV	giorno	mese	anno	S	KK	PI	AA	MM A	GD	COLI	DIV	
1																								
1																								
1																								

tipo scheda	numero parto	data svezzamento			numero svezzati	peso in kg.	cod el.	maschi tatuati		femmine tatuate		linea genetica		codice svezz.
		giorno	mese	anno				da	a	da	a	maschi	femmine	
19	20 21	22 23	24 25	26 27	28 29	30 31	32	33 34 35	36 37	38 39	40 41	42	43	80
2														

scrofa: razza   numero   tat.   da non accoppiare con i seguenti verri:

razza	numero	tat.	razza	numero	tat.	razza	numero	tat.	razza	numero	tat.	razza	numero	tat.	razza	numero	tat.

ni 039

---

sildamin®

p.a. **G. Piero Piatto**
Servizio tecnico
commerciale

25030 Torbole Casaglia
Brescia
Via Verdi, 1
Telefono 030.2787297

Sildamin spa
alimenti e sistemi
per la zootecnia

27010 Sostegno di Spessa
Pavia
Telefono 0382.79176 (5 linee)
Telex 321107 Sildam I

Maltinti
Kitchen Furniture
台所用家具
Italy 1985
Signo
AD, D/Heinz Waibl

Maltinti spa
Cucine d'Arredamento

Cap. soc. 600.000.000 i.v.
CCIAA 67300 trib. 2187
Codice fiscale 00108530478

51030 Serravalle (PT)
Via Provinciale
Vecchia Lucchese 39
Telefono 0573/51203/4

c.f.

Conto provvigioni n.   del

VI inviamo il conto provvigioni per il periodo   come da conteggi già compilati sulle copie-fatture trasmesseci

1. ordine diretto   n. fattura   data   importi merce   importi provvigioni
2. a 1/2 ns.

Maltinti spa
Cucine d'Arredamento

Cap. soc. 600 000 000 i.v.
CCIAA 67300 trib. 2187
Codice fiscale 00108530478

51030 Serravalle (PT)
Via Provinciale
Vecchia Lucchese 39
Telefono 0573/51203/4

Serravalle,

Maltinti spa
Cucine d'Arredamento

Cap. soc. 600.000.000 i.v.
CCIAA 67300 trib. 2187
Codice fiscale 00108530478

51030 Serravalle (PT)
Via Provinciale
Vecchia Lucchese 39
Telefono 0573/51203/4

Maltinti spa
Cucine d'Arredamento

Roberto Maltinti   51030 Serravalle (PT)
Via Provinciale
Vecchia Lucchese 39
Telefono 0573/51203/4
Codice fiscale 00108530478

Maltinti
Kitchen Furniture
台所用家具
Italy 1985
Signo
AD, D/Heinz Waibl

BGH

Boris Garfunkel e Hijos SA
Inmobiliaria Comercial
Financiera e Industrial

Brasil 731
Buenos Aires
T.E. 26 6001/10
Cables Garfunkijo
Telex 121548

BGH

Boris Garfunkel e Hijos SA
Inmobiliaria Comercial
Financiera e Industrial

Brasil 731
Buenos Aires
T.E. 26 6001/10
Cables Garfunkijo
Telex 121548

Orden de Compra

Número

Fecha

Señor/es

Proveedor N° Sirvase indicar este número
en la documentación remitida a BGH.

Requisición N°

Muy señor/es nuestro/s:
Sirvase entregar en las condiciones estipuladas más abajo, y según cláusulas que
figuran al dorso y que se consideran parte integrante de esta orden de compra, la
mercadería cuya espesificación se detalla.

Lugar de Entrega

Condición Pago

Imputación

*Código	Cantidad	Detalle	Precio Unit.	Total

*Sirvase indicar
remito y en la me
mediante sello ch

BGH   SICOM

SICOM Sistemas de Comunicaciones
Sociedad Anónima Industrial
Comercial y Financiera

Brasil 731
Buenos Aires
T.E. 26 6001/10

Recibimos
de SICOM Sistemas de Comunicaciones SACIFA
la cantidad de pesos

Número

Fecha

Son $

Firma

Proveedor

GFP
Advertising
広告業
Italy 1973
Giulio Cittato
AD,D/Giulio Cittato

98 99

Letts of London Pty Ltd.
Distributors of Diaries and
Address Books
日記帳・住所録の販売
Australia 1986
WM de Majo Associates
AD,D/WM de Majo
A/Tony Forster

Three famous Diarists

John Letts founded the business in the Royal Exchange in 1796
and published the first Commercial Diary in 1812.
Since then six generations have actively directed the business.

Letts of London Pty Ltd

NBL Distribution Centre
34 Wyndham Street, Alexandria, Sydney, Australia/Telephone: 699 6566
Postal Address: Box 239, P.O. Redfern, 2016
Telex: AA24573 Cables: ONOTO Sydney

Audio-visual and Film Company
オーディオ・ヴィジュアルおよび映画製作
Sweden 1969
Olle Eksell Design
D/Olle Eksell

AV Producenterna AB

Peter Günz
Lyckostigen 14, 183 50 Täby
08 - 768 46 61, 768 46 62
Postgiro 68 10 15 - 4   Bankgiro 402 - 8635
Handelsbanken

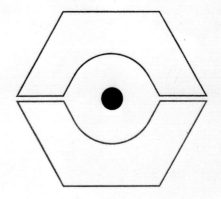

WNYC
Public Radio and
Television Company
公共ラジオ・テレビ会社
USA 1981
Pentagram Design
AD/Colin Forbes
D/Dan Friedman

The Communications Service
of the City of New York
John Beck, Director

One Centre Street
New York, NY 10007
212 566-2113

A member of:
National Public Radio
Public Broadcasting Service

AM83   *FM94*   *TV31*

KERA Channel 13
Public Television Station
公共テレビ局
USA 1985
Richards Brock Miller
Mitchell & Associates
AD/Steve Miller, Scott Paramski
D, A/Scott Paramski

KERA Channel 13
3000 Harry Hines Boulevard
Dallas, Texas 75201
214/871-1390 Metro 263-3151

13

The Solar Film
Film Production
映画製作
USA 1980
Saul Bass/Herb Yager & Associates
D/Saul & Elaine Bass
A/Elaine & Saul Bass
C/Robert Redford

The Solar Film
Film Production
映画製作
USA 1980
Saul Bass/Herb Yager & Associates
D/Saul & Elaine Bass
A/Elaine & Saul Bass
C/Robert Redford

Geffen Records
Entertainment Industry
エンターテイメント産業
USA 1981
Saul Bass/Herb Yager & Associates
D, A/Saul Bass, G. Dean Smith

104 105

9126 Sunset Boulevard   75 Rockefeller Plaza
Los Angeles California 90069   New York New York 10019
Telephone 213 278 9010   Telephone 212 484 7170

Esprit de Corp.
Fashion Company
ファッション会社
USA 1984
Esprit Design
AD, D, A/Tamotsu Yagi

Esprit de Corp.
Fashion Company
ファッション会社
USA 1985
Esprit Design
AD, D, A/Tamotsu Yagi

106 107

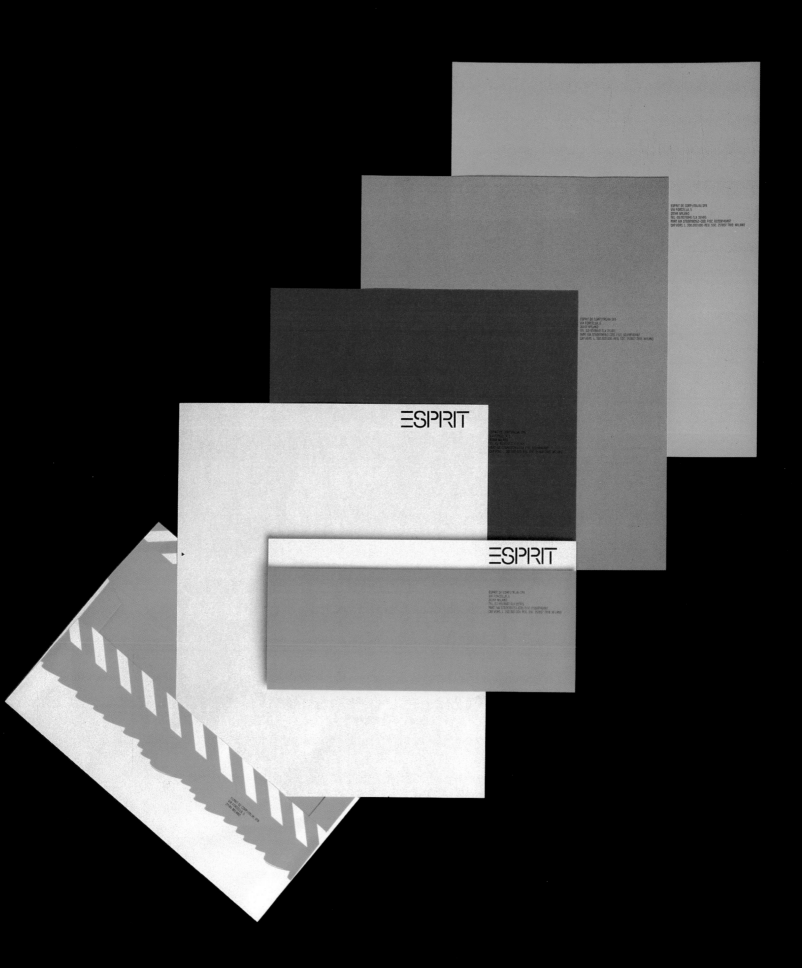

The Milestone Hotel
ホテル
USA 1985
Pirtle Design
AD/Woody Pirtle, Kenny Garrison
D,A/Kenny Garrison
C/Simpson Paper Company

THE MILESTONE HOTEL   93 PARLIAMENT STREET   TORONTO, CANADA MSA IVI 410 366 2788

Simpson Protocol Writing, Soft Blue, Wove, Sub 24. Lithographed one color, duotone and metallic foil emboss.

Mandarin Oriental Hotel Group
ホテル・グループ
Hong Kong 1985
Pentagram Design
D/Alan Fletcher, Tessa Boo Mitford

108 109

THE MANDARIN
HONG KONG

The Mandarin, 5 Connaught Road, Central, PO Box 2623, Hong Kong
Telephone (5) 220111. Telex 73653 MANDA HX
Facsimile (5) 297978. Cable MANDARIN HONG KONG

Mandarin Oriental Hotel Group

Schweizerische Bundesbahnen
Freight Transport
貨物輸送
Switzerland 1974
Kurt Wirth
AD, D, A/Kurt Wirth

Schweizerische Bundesbahnen
Chemins de fer fédéraux suisses
Ferrovie federali svizzere

Kommerzieller Dienst Güterverkehr
Service commercial trafic marchandises
Servizio commerciale traffico merci

SBB CFF FFS

Telegramm
Télégramme
Telegramma   Tarif Bern

Telefon   031 60 11 11
Direkt

PC   30 - 193

Ihre Nachricht vom
Votre correspondance du
Vostra corrispondenza del

Ihr Zeichen
Votre référence
Vostro riferimento

Unser Zeichen
Notre référence
Nostro riferimento

Sachbearbeiter
Traité par
Funzionario

3000 Bern
Mittelstrasse 43

SBB 2139 II 72 15 000

Los Angeles Olympic
Organizing Committee
ロサンゼルス・オリンピック組織委員会
USA 1983
Arnold Schwartzman Productions Inc.
D/Arnold Schwartzman
A/James Robie Studio

The Los Angeles Olympic Organizing Committee
Los Angeles, California 90084 USA
Telephone (213) 209-1984
Telex: 194694—(International) 4720482

Apple Computer, Inc.
コンピュータ会社
USA 1984
Apple Creative Services
AD/Tom Suiter
D/Ron Harsh

Apple Computer, Inc.
20525 Mariani Avenue
Cupertino, California 95014
408 973-2121 or 996-1010

コンピュータ会社
Apple Creative Services
AD/Tom Suiter
D/Ron Harsh

Compucare Services
Data Management
情報サービス業
USA 1985
Richardson or Richardson
AD,D/Forrest & Valerie Richardson

CompuCare

Services, Inc.

Data Management
Sales/Service/Consultation

1659 South Westwood
Suite B
Mesa, Arizona 85202
602-838-7626

Next, Inc.
Computer Manufacturer
コンピュータ・メーカー
USA 1986
Paul Rand
AD, D/Paul Rand

NeXT, Inc.
3475 Deer Creek Road
Palo Alto, California 94304

415 424 0200
415 424 0476 (Fax)

Next, Inc.
Computer Manufacturer
コンピュータ・メーカー
USA 1986
Paul Rand
AD, D/Paul Rand

AIGA
Institute for the Promotion
of Design
デザイン団体
USA 1965
Paul Rand
AD, D, A/Paul Rand

AIGA

The American Institute of Graphic Arts
1059 Third Avenue
New York 10021
Plaza 2-0813 area code 212

Air Canada
航空会社
Canada 1977
George Tscherny Inc.
AD, D/George Tscherny

Sky America
Travelling Exhibit
移動展示
USA 1975
Chermayeff & Geismar Associates
AD, D/Ivan Chermayeff

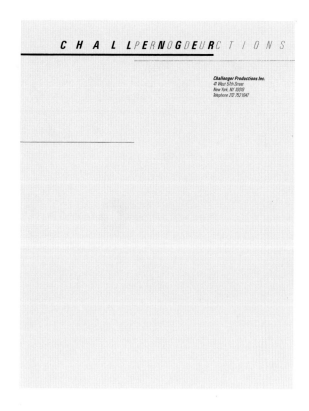

Challenger Production
Film Production Company
映画製作
USA 1984
Gonda Design, Inc.
AD, D/Tomás Gonda

Corporacion Agbar, S.A.
Finance of Water-related Businesses
水関連事業ファイナンス
Spain 1983
Enric Huguet
D/Enric Huguet

Centro de Textos Electronico, S.A.
Photo Composition Using Informatics
コンピュータ写植
Spain 1986
Pla-Narbona
AD, D/Pla-Narbona

Novapress AG
Magazine Publishing
出版
Switzerland 1984
Gottschalk + Ash International
D/Fritz Gottschalk

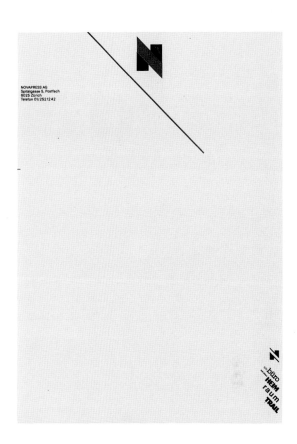

Symbiosis, Inc.
Film Production Company
映画製作
USA 1981
Rudolph de Harak & Assoc.
D/Rudolph de Harak

Alcan Aluminum
アルミ会社
Canada 1984
Rolf Harder & Assoc.
AD/Rolf Harder, Gloria Ménard
D/Rolf Harder
A/Rolf Harder, Leo Schweizer

Construzioni Civili Industriali
Civil Construction
土木建設会社
Italy
Unidesign
AD, D/Walter Ballmer

AUTOMACSA
Garage
自動車修理業
Switzerland 1982
Oberholzer Tagli Cevio
AD, D/Sabina Oberholzer, Renato Tagli

Lisney Associates
Architects
建築
England 1980
Pentagram Design
D/David Hillman, Nancy Williams
A/Richard Draper

Datalink Zürich
Computer Services AG
コンピュータ・サービス会社
Switzerland 1976
Odermatt & Tissi
AD, D, A/Siegfried Odermatt

Gianni Boselli
Furniture Store
家具販売店
Italy 1974
Giulio Cittato
AD, D/Giulio Cittato

GEM Consulting Co., Ltd.
Business Consulting Firm
経営コンサルティング
Japan 1986
Igarashi Studio
AD/Takenobu Igarashi
D/Yukimi Sasago

arredamenti   castello 3540
boselli   venezia
               telefono 27374

GEM Consulting Co., Ltd.
6-7-5 Minami Aoyama
Minato-ku, Tokyo
107 Japan
Phone 03-407-2356

ジェムコンサルティング株式会社
東京都港区南青山6-7-5
郵便番号107
電話 03-407-2356

TELEVISION
AUSTRALIA
Satellite Systems Limited

Prestel Headquarters
British Post Office
Alder House
1 Aldersgate Street
London EC1A 1AL

Telephone: (01) 248 4102
International Code: (+441)

Prestel and the Prestel symbol
are trademarks of the
Post Office viewdata service

2nd Floor, 22 Sir John Young Crescent, Woolloomooloo NSW 2011
Telephone: (02) 356 2077   Fax: (02) 357 1704   Telex: 73804
Incorporated in NSW

British Telecom: Prestel
Computer Data via Television
データ通信会社
England 1978
Pentagram Design
D/Mervyn Kurlansky, Lora Starling

Television Australia Satellite Systems Ltd.
Cummunications Systems Consultants
コミュニケーション・システム・コンサルティング
Australia 1986
Raymond Bennett Design Associates
AD/Raymond Bennett
D/Ingo Voss

The Israeli Sinfonietta
Orchestra
オーケストラ
Israel 1983
Yarom Vardimon
AD, D/Yarom Vardimon

Graphis Press Corp.
Publishing Company
出版社
Switzerland 1979
Graphis, Zürich Switzerland
AD, D, A/Walter Herdeg

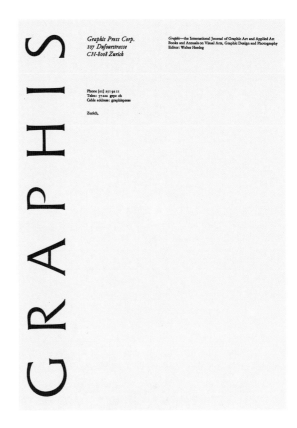

Southern California Graphics
Printing Company
印刷会社
USA
John Cleveland Inc.
AD/John Cleveland
D/Michael Skjei

CFD
Council of Fashion Designer's, Tokyo
東京ファッションデザイナー協議会
Japan 1985
Ikko Tanaka Design Studio
AD, D/Ikko Tanaka

Olympic Art Festival
ロサンゼルス・オリンピック芸術祭
USA 1983
Arnold Schwartzman Productions Inc.
AD, D/Arnold Schwartzman
A/James Robie Studio
C/Los Angeles Olympic Games
Organizing Commitee

Jewish Olympic Games
ユダヤ・オリンピック大会
Israel 1977
Dan Reisinger
AD, D, A/Dan Reisinger
C/Maccabiah Games Committee

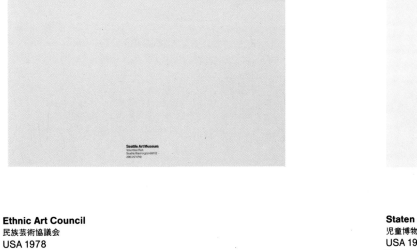

Ethnic Art Council
民族芸術協議会
USA 1978
Rickabaugh Design
AD/Robin & Heidi Rickabaugh
D/Robin Rickabaugh
C/Seattle Art Museum

Staten Island Children's Museum
児童博物館
USA 1986
Works
AD, D/Keith Godard

Mobil Oil Corporation
Television Presentation
テレビ番組
USA 1975
Chermayeff & Geismar Associates
AD, D, A/Ivan Chermayeff

Mobil Oil Corporation
Free Concert Series
フリー・コンサート・シリーズ
USA 1979
Chermayeff & Geismar Associates
AD, D, A/Ivan Chermayeff

Mobil Oil Corporation
Television Presentation
テレビ番組
USA 1980
Chermayeff & Geismar Associates
AD, D, A/Ivan Chermayeff

Mobil Oil Corporation
Free Concert Series
フリー・コンサート・シリーズ
USA 1971
Chermayeff & Geismar Associates
AD, D, A/Ivan Chermayeff

Mobil Oil Corporation
Television Presentation
テレビ番組
USA 1982
Chermayeff & Geismar Associates
AD, D, A/Ivan Chermayeff

White House Conference
on Children
ホワイトハウス児童協議会
USA 1970
Chermayeff & Geismar Associates
AD, D, A/Ivan Chermayeff

Mobil Oil Corporation
Television Presentation
テレビ番組
USA 1981
Chermayeff & Geismar Associates
AD, D, A/Ivan Chermayeff

White House Conference
on Youth
ホワイトハウス青少年協議会
USA 1971
Chermayeff & Geismar Associates
AD, D/Tom Geismar

Minneapolis Children's Medical Center
ミネアポリス児童医療センター
USA 1984
Seitz Yamamoto Moss
D/Aimee Hucek

Yosemite Institute
Natural Sciences Educational
Organization for the Young
自然科学教育協会
USA 1985
Akagi Design
AD, D/Doug Akagi

Portland Museum
ポートランド博物館
USA 1983
Images
AD/Julius Friedman
D/Julius Friedman, Walter McCord

Portland Museum
2308 Portland Avenue
Louisville, Kentucky 40212
(502) 776-7678

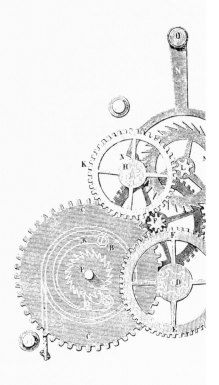

Portland Museum
ポートランド博物館
USA 1983
Images
AD/Julius Friedman
D/Julius Friedman, Walter McCord

Pennsylvania Folkart Museum
ペンシルバニア民芸博物館
USA 1985
Pirtle Design
AD/Woody Pirtle, Kenny Garrison
D,A/Kenny Garrison
C/Simpson Paper Company

126 127

PENNSYLVANIA FOLKART MUSEUM

7 Plymouth Circle

Philadelphia, Pennsylvania 19103

(215) 780-4770

Simpson Protocol Writing, Warm Tan, Laid, Sub 24. Four color process over opaque white. Photographs–Collection of the Museum of American Folk Art.

The Glenwood School
デザイン学校
USA 1982
Pirtle Design
AD, D, A/Woody Pirtle

Mills College
Women's College
女子大学
USA 1982
Pentagram Design
D/Neil Shakery

MILLS

COLLEGE

Mills College
Women's College
女子大学
USA 1982
Pentagram Design
D/Neil Shakery

Het Muziektheater
The Music Theater in Amsterdam
アムステルダム音楽劇場
Netherlands 1986
TD Associates
D/Gijsbert Dijker

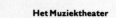

Het Muziektheater

Postadres:
Postbus 16822
1001 RH Amsterdam

Bezoekadres:
Waterlooplein 22
1011 PG Amsterdam

Het Muziektheater
Tel. 020-551 89 11
De Nederlandse Opera
Tel. 020-551 89 22
Het Nationale Ballet
Tel. 020-551 89 11

Telex Muzth 13572
Bank 44 42 22 111
Postbank 50 40 573

Dallas Opera
オペラ
USA 1977
The Richards Group
AD, D, A/Woody Pirtle

130 131

**Dallas
Opera**

3000 Turtle Creek Plaza
Dallas, Texas 75219
General Office (214) 528-9850
Ticket Office (214) 528-3200
Cable: Dalopera

Plato Karayanis
General Director

Nicola Rescigno
Artistic Director

Doug Akagi United States
Recognizing that stationery is never seen blank, we design letterheads on a grid created with the client's typewriter or computer printer. We also design the body of the letter itself, recommending the margins, width, paragraph treatment and line spacing between the date, the salutation and the closing. For clients with only typewriters, we put small (almost invisible) guide dots to aid the typist in positioning each element of the letter. The final detail is a small hairline printed two-thirds up from the bottom and bleeding off the left side. By folding the bottom of the sheet up to this line and the top portion down, the letterhead is folded in equal thirds.
When making the design presentation, we have a typed letter reproduced on a clear film positive to demonstrate how the letterhead appears in its completed form.

D.C. Stipp United States
The letterhead is always a challenge. It's the fun of taking different forms of the same elements and working with them within the limitations of stationery. It's trying to push the limits as far as you can and still maintain a vehicle to carry a letter. The South Street Celebration stationery was solved with this in mind, as it was designed in a festive way, following the nature of this special event.

Gerry Rosentsieg United States
The importance of the letterhead is obvious. It tells the recipient more than your name, address and telephone number. The letterhead describes the company. The designer's job is to make the letterhead distinctive as well as descriptive, to give it the personality of the business it represents and to insure that the design is appropriate. This means that the designer must have as much information as possible.
Especially difficult is the new business stationery, where a clear cut personality does not yet exist. In some cases, the graphics, paper and color choices give the business its personality. This type of assignment can be the most difficult and the most gratifying.

Heather Cooper Canada
A letterhead should be memorable, appropriate, and be a reflection of the individual or corporate personality.

Marianne Tombaugh United States
In creating the letterhead/corporate image for The Hay (advertising) Agency, several factors were considered. We wanted an image of class and professionalism. An image that juxtaposed creative innovation with sound business acumen. An image that would project well to our clients — from real estate developers to bankers. From computer companies to industrial lubricant manufacturers.
And since graphic designers are very subject to design trends, special attention needs to be paid in creating a corporate identity that is not only pre-emptive, but also timeless. The life span of a letterhead/corporate image should equal the life of the company. An updated look or redesign should never be necessary. Therefore, design trends in colors, formats, type and paper can soon become dated if they are not chosen with a sensitivity and awareness to design history and cycles.

April Greiman United States
Letterheads for your personal use... 'the hardest job in the world to design.'
Letterheads in your business world... 'mostly insensitive and typographically missing opportunities to communicate important information and messages.'
Letterhead design in this age of computers...'we do the 'roughs' on computer.'

Louis Dorfsman United States
'When a designer designs a letterhead for himself (or herself) or for close friends, it poses special problems.'
'On the one hand in designing personal stationery one reaches for the 'moon'...for the ultimate...for something so superb that one's comtemporaries will respond with envy — while one gloats over this design victory.
But it rarely happens that designers can outdo themselves for themselves. So we retreat to a safe position of producing a tasteful, conservative typographic solution which does not expose one to criticism but merely says 'here's a business-like piece of stationery sensitively done but not really an example of how good I am — how I save my real talents for others.'
However when designing for friends I try my best for more style and concepts...Because it carries someone elses name on the stationery, one feels absolved of blame if the results are't outstanding. Its called a 'cop-out' in English.

Richard Moore United States

Letterhead design is no different than any other type of graphic design in most respects — the design should visually express the personality of the client, whether it is for an individual or a large corporation. However, with the design of the letterheads, there is an opportunity to go beyond what is printed, and use what the typist will later add. The empty compositions we see in books such as this are often beautiful — but incomplete. Other than the designers and the client's secretaries, few people will ever see an untyped letterhead. By treating the typing format as a design element a more cohesive visual impression can be achieved.

To create stationery which integrates typing with the design of the letterhead, visual cues must be provided, such as small dots and dashes, to indicate typing positions and fold marks for the typist. The results are usually worth the effort.

Tommy Steele United States

In the graphic design business a letterhead and business card is how we advertise for ourselves. It is an image maker and an expression of who we are. More emphasis needs to be put on selling this kind of identity to a client. It is as important as the product he sells.

Unfortunately most of the experimental letterheads we design are for ourselves. But that is our job as designers — to elevate people's tastes. We have an excuse to design new letterheads when our old ones run out. Gotta keep current.

Marilyn Worseldine United States

My last name is not the easiet to spell. Over the years I collected mail addressed to me with the craziest mistakes.

It seemed a humorous idea to apply this collection to my letterhead...using the correct spelling, printed in a second color, just above the address. Worselwhat?

Miranda Moss United States

The letterheads we design are part of a total corporate identity package. In some corporations the business correspondence is the prime conveyence of the image and in others it is the first marketing tool that a client will have to reach a potential customer. We have found that introducing a full color symbol or graphic treatment gets a lot of attention and creates a memorable impression.

Cynthia H. Marsh United States

For myself, I feel my letterhead and stationery should change often. The visual impact should give the viewer some sense of the influences that are effecting my life at this point in time.

Cary Staples United States

Letterhead design is a very important aspect of a campany's corporate identity, usually being the first glimpse inside by an outsider. The letterhead is not just a piece of paper with a name and address, it reflects the systematic process that a company uses to communicate with the outside world.

The initial impact of the letterhead is visual, however. If functional considerations have not been carefully thought out, the visual impact will not be as strong. Functionally, the letterhead should be easy to use and take into consideration; layout, the various kinds of formating programs or wordprocessors that the company is using; stock, the paper that was specified should be available with tractor feed if mail merge programs are being employed; typefaces, the typeface should be chosen to be compatable with those of the typewriters or printers available. In addition, legal, federal and budgetary constraints must also be taken into consideration.

In addition to the practical analysis of the company, a philosophical analysis needs to be done. Only when the designer discovers those unique aspects that the company wishes to project and merges them with the practical considerations does he have the information to create a solution that will be appropriate and unique.

"The solution to the problem lies within the problem itself."

My letterhead was designed to meet my specific needs; it had to be inexpensive to print and remain versatile as I needed to use it for everything from letters to invoices to resumes. The final design is a play on my last name "staples". The staples are not only used as a design device but when there is more then one page they fasten the pages. The design is a single card so that there was only one printing. The card is spray glued to letterhead stock and cut down to form the business card. The phone numbers are at the bottom so they can be cut off when the card is attached to an envelope. The letter is horizontal because I liked the typography that this format created and the short letters that I write look better. This system has worked very well as it provides the flexibility that I need, yet I think the final "look" is cohesive and implies visual creative problem solving, which is what I do.

The Canine Company
Dog Groomer
犬訓練会社
USA 1985
Richardson or Richardson
AD, D/Forrest & Valerie Richardson

Hedgehog Promotions
Public Relations and
Media Consultant
広告・メディア・コンサルタント
Australia 1980
Ken Cato Design Company
AD,D/Ken Cato
A/Mark Littler

Tom Kummer
Equestrian Guide
乗馬指導
Switzerland 1986
Oberholzer Tagli Cevio
AD, D/Sablna Oberholzer, Renato Tagli

Tom Kummer
guida equestre

CH-6653 Verscio
tel. 093 81 25 06

Verscio

Carlos Navajas
Location Photographer
写真家
Spain 1984
Medina Design
AD, D, A/Fernando Medina

Carlos Navajas
Fotógrafo.
Vinaroz 16-B-3-11
28002 Madrid Spain
Tel. 415 50 35

Sunny Side Up Inc.
Japanese Film Production in USA
在米日本映画製作会社
USA 1984
Glenn Parsons Design
AD, D, A/Glenn Parsons

SUNNY SIDE UP INCORPORATED
6115 San Vincente Boulevard
Los Angeles, California 90048
213 938-7700
TLX-181149 WEST-LSA

American Transfers & Tours
Bus Service-charter
バス・チャーター業
USA 1986
Krause & Young Inc.
AD,D/Bob Young
A/David Bell

138 139

5646 Milton · Suite 120 · Dallas, Tx. · 75206 · 214-368-2077

Dick Wilson
Humorous Illustrator
イラストレーター
USA 1982
Vita Design
AD,D/Vita Otrubova
A/Dick Wilson

DICK WILSON
humorous illustrations

120 Belgrave Avenue
San Francisco ∗ California 94117
telephone 415·821 4818

The Big Black Chicken
Direct Mail Marketing
通信販売
USA 1985
Market Sights Inc.
AD, A/Marilyn Worseldine

140 141

The Big Black Chicken
1231 Thirtieth Street, Northwest
Washington, District of Columbia 20007
Telephone 202-965-4325

Janet K. Harnsberger MD
Pediatrician
小児科医
USA 1983
La Pine/O'Very, Inc.
AD,D,A/Julia La Pine, Traci O'Very Covey

Janet K. Harnsberger MD
Pediatric Gastroenterology and Nutrition

Cottonwood Medical Towers
250 East 5770 South, Suite 210B
Murray, Utah 84107

Cheshire Cat
Bookstore
書店
USA 1985
La Pine/O'Very, Inc.
AD,D/Julia La Pine, Traci O'Very Covey
A/Celia Stratton

169 South
Bluff Street
St. George,
Utah 84770
801-628-4265

Sam Angeloff
Copywriter
コピーライター
USA 1986
Rick Eiber Design
AD, D/Rick Eiber

Antonello Tiracchi
Photographer
写真家
Italy 1980
Rinaldo Cutini
D/Rinaldo Cutini

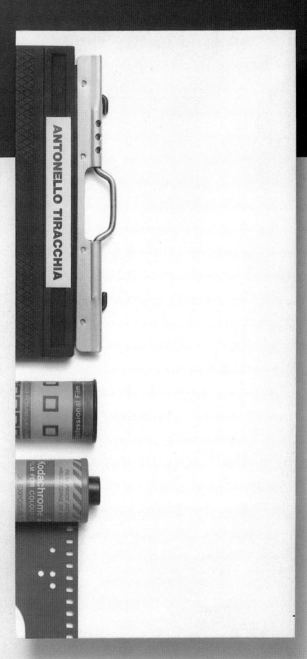

21 Via Plinio 00193 Roma
Telefono 3599595

DISTRIBUTING CORPORATION

AIC
12110 SHERMAN WAY
NORTH HOLLYWOOD
CALIFORNIA 91605

12110 SHERMAN WAY
NORTH HOLLYWOOD
CALIFORNIA 91605
(818) 982-0514

AIC

The Slide Gallery
Slide Production Services
スライド製作サービス業
USA 1985
Rick Eiber Design
AD, D/Rick Eiber

146 147

International Puppet Festival
国際操り人形祭
Australia 1983
Barrie Tucker Design Pty Ltd.
AD, D/Barrie Tucker
A/Robert Marshall

ASSITEJ Australia
World Congress for Youth Theater
青少年劇場世界会議
Australia 1986
Barrie Tucker Design Pty Ltd.
AD, D/Barrie Tucker
A/Mark Janetzki

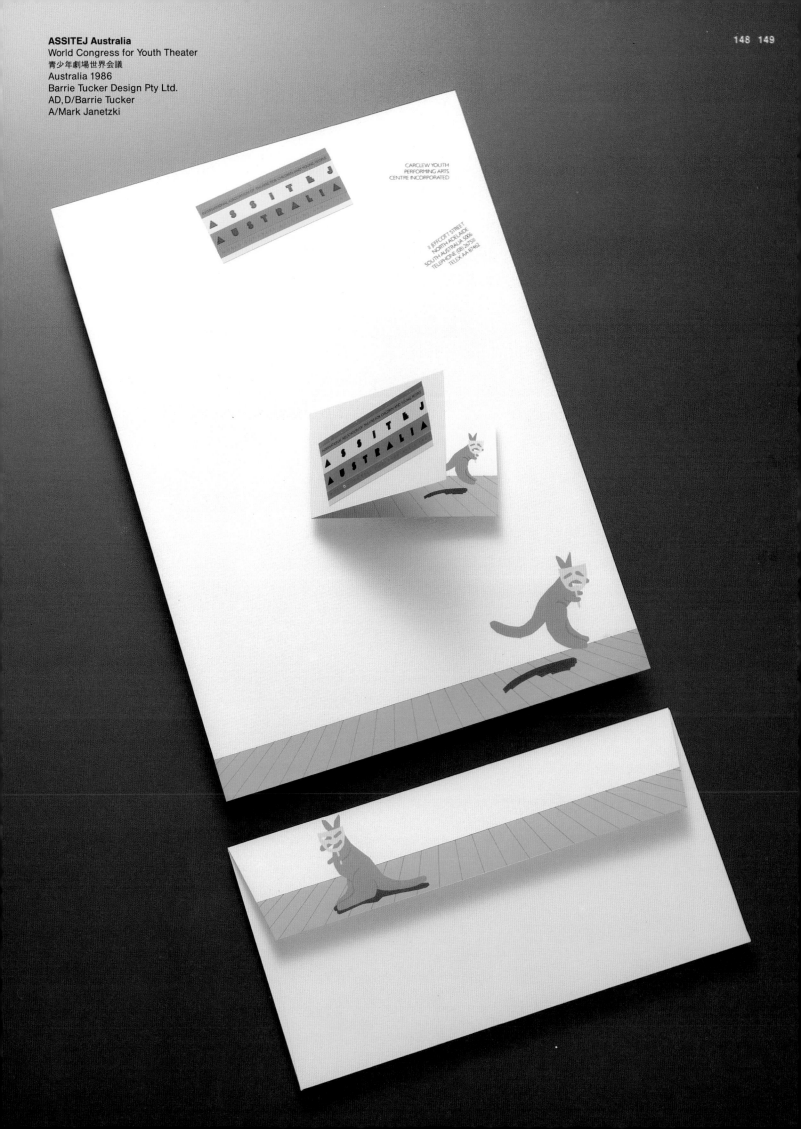

John Cliff & Associates
Audio Visual Production
オーディオ・ビジュアル製作
Australia 1979
Ken Cato Design Company
AD, D/Ken Cato
A/Bob Haberfield

John Cliff & Associates

Multi-image Audio Visual Production
611 St Kilda Road Melbourne Victoria 3004 Australia
Telephone 03 51 8734

Lena Gan
Illustrator
イラストレーター
Australia
Ken Cato Design Company
AD, D/Ken Cato
A/Lena Gan

LENA GAN

8/43 ARMADALE STREET, ARMADALE, VICTORIA 3143, AUSTRALIA, TELEPHONE 500 0710

Susan Crutcher
Film Editing
映画編集
USA 1986
Michael Schwab Design
AD, D, A/Michael Schwab

3918 20TH STREET
San Francisco 9 4 1 1 4
映画編集

SUSAN CRUTCHER
film editing

Telephone
415 552 4691

International Postproduction
Film Production Company
映画製作
England 1985
Michael Peters + Partners
AD, D/Glenn Tutssel

INTERNATIONAL POSTPRODUCTION
99 FRESTON ROAD, LONDON W11 4BD
TELEPHONE 01 221 9041
TELEX: 297247, FAX: 01 221 9399

DIRECTORS: WILLIAM WARBURTON (CHAIRMAN),
MAURICE HAMBLIN (MANAGING),
BRIAN CARROLL, JOHN GRIFFIN, JOHN HORNER
VAT REGISTRATION NO: 251 45 866 1
REGISTERED OFFICE: COMMONWEALTH HOUSE,
NEW OXFORD STREET, LONDON WC1A 1PF
REGISTERED IN ENGLAND NO: 985326

A MEMBER OF THE WESTWAY GROUP OF COMPANIES

South Street Seaport
Developer
地域開発会社
USA 1984
Richards Brock Miller
Mitchell & Associates
AD, D/D.C.Stipp
C/Rouse Campany

✾ Dedication Celebration Office ✾ 19 Fulton Street ✾ New York, New York 10038 ✾ 212-SEA-PORT ✾

地域開発会社
USA 1984
Richards Brock Miller
Mitchell & Associates
AD, D/D.C.Stipp
C/Rouse Campany

Ostrobotnia Restaurant
レストラン
Finland 1985
Veistola Oy
AD,D,A/Jukka Veistola

154 155

Oy Botta Ab, Töölönkatu 3, 00I00 Helsinki, puh. 446 940 (Toimisto puh. 494 204)

Phoenician Explorations
Searching for Sunken Treasure
沈潜財宝探査
USA 1980
Heather Cooper Illustration & Design
D/Heather Cooper, Lawrence Finn
A/Heather Cooper

PHOENICIAN
EXPLORATIONS
A Limited Partnership

Director
R. F. Marx
330 Thyme Street
Satellite Beach
Florida 32937, U.S.A.
Telephone: (305) 777-2061

General Partner
Phoenician Explorations Inc.
401 Bay Street, Suite 2400
Toronto, Canada M5H 2Y4
Telephone: (416) 367-1290
TWX. 610 491 1762

Limited Partners
R. M. Barford, Toronto
B. M. Benitz, Toronto
R. A. N. Bonnycastle, Calgary
R. Burns, Toronto
M. C. J. Cowpland, Ottawa
H. Cooper, Toronto
Michel de Bourbon de Parme,
Paris
P. D'Orsay, Toronto
J. C. Eaton, Toronto
B. M. Flood, Toronto
R. A. Gunn, Toronto
A. Hodgson, Montreal
V. Hodgson, Montreal
P. V. Huggler, Tokyo
R. M. Ivey, London, Ontario
L. P. Kelly, New York
M. M. Koerner, Toronto
R. J. Lawrence, Toronto
D. Lindsay, Johannesburg
C. B. Loewen, Toronto
H. de Maigret, Philadelphia
P. de Maigret, Philadelphia
W. L. Matthews, Toronto
C. Naess, London, England
M. J. Needham, Toronto
M. F. B. Nesbitt, Winnipeg
P. C. Ondaatje, Toronto
R. J. Opekar, Toronto
A. G. Quasha, New York
L. L. Reynolds. Philadelphia
F. M. Rolph, Montreal
J. Rupert, Stellenbosch
J. C. Rykert, Toronto
N. J. Short, Toronto
W. W. Siebens, Calgary
G. M. Soloway, Toronto
S. H. Wallace, Vancouver
G. T. Watchorn, Toronto
D. C. Webster, Toronto
L. C. Webster, Montreal
R. H. Webster, Montreal

Imprints
Importers and Distributors of
Paper Products
紙製品輸入販売
Canada 1984
Heather Cooper Illustration & Design
D, A/Heather Cooper, Cara-Lynn Rumack

156 157

IMPRINTS
124 Newbold Ct.
London, Ontario
Canada N6E 1Z7
(519) 685-1112

Helmut Swozilek
Archaeologist
考古学者
Austria 1979
Harry Metzler
AD, D, A/Harry Metzler

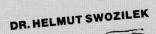

DR. HELMUT SWOZILEK

A-6911 LOCHAU

Schlagheck & Schultes Design
Design
デザイン
W. Germany 1980
Mendell & Oberer
D/Pierre Mendell

158 159

Schlagheck Schultes Design GmbH
Reichenhaller Straße 48
8000 München 90
Telefon 0 89/66 20 37

Geschäftsführer:
Prof. Norbert Schlagheck
VDID DWB
und Herbert H. Schultes VDID DWB

Registergericht
München HR B 52212
Hypobank Olching BLZ 700 255 01
Konto-Nr. 4 520 123 720

Baker's Brands Flavors
Baking Industry
Flavour manufacturer
菓子製造
USA 1984
The Graphics Studio
AD,D,A/Gerry Rosentswieg

Baker's Brands Flavors
Baking Industry
Flavour manufacturer
菓子製造
USA 1984
The Graphics Studio
AD,D,A/Gerry Rosentswieg

Old Poodle Dog
Restaurant
レストラン
USA 1982
Gerald Reis & Company
AD, D, A/Gerald Reis

Shangrila Hotel
ホテル
USA 1987
Dyer/Kahn, Inc.
AD/Rod Dyer
D,A/Clive Piercy

1301 OCEAN AVE., SANTA MONICA, CALIF. 90401 (213) 394-2791 TLX: 182091

The Famous Computer Cafe
Computer Information Talk Show
コンピュータ情報のトーク・ショウ
USA 1987
Dyer/Kahn, Inc.
AD/Rod Dyer
D,A/Clive Piercy

THE FAMOUS
COMPUTER CAFE

1322 Second St., Suite 24
Santa Monica, CA 90401

213 394•7242

Menu

A PRODUCTION OF SOFTV, INC.

Marketing Solutions
Marketing Consultancy
マーケティング・コンサルティング
England 1982
David Pocknell's Co.
AD, D/David Pocknell

MARKETING SOLUTIONS

Marketing
Solutions
Limited
70 Salusbury Road
Queen's Park
London NW6 6NU
Telephone 01-624 6090

MARKETING SOLUTIONS

Marketing
Solutions
Limited
70 Salusbury Road
Queen's Park
London NW6 6NU
Telephone 01-624 6090

MARKETING SOLUTIONS

Marketing
Solutions
Limited
70 Salusbury Road Queen's Park London NW6 6NU
Telephone 01-624 6090

Sportsmen in Business
Sports Personalities Agency
スポーツ・パーソナリティ・エージェンシー
England 1982
David Pocknell's Co.
AD, D/David Pocknell

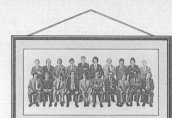

SPORTSMEN IN BUSINESS

70 Salusbury Road, Queen's Park, London NW6 6NU
Telephone: 01-624 6090

Company Registration No. 1509834
Directors:- David Bryant, Willie Carson, John Lowe, Mick Mills,
Jonathan Crisp, David Drakes

SPORTSMEN IN BUSINESS

70 Salusbury Road, Queen's Park, London NW6 6NU
Telephone: 01-624 6090

Jonjo O'Neill

Emily Aronson
Food Innovation
フード・イノベーション
USA 1985
Lou Dorfsman Inc.
AD,D/Lou Dorfsman
A/Yasuo Kubota

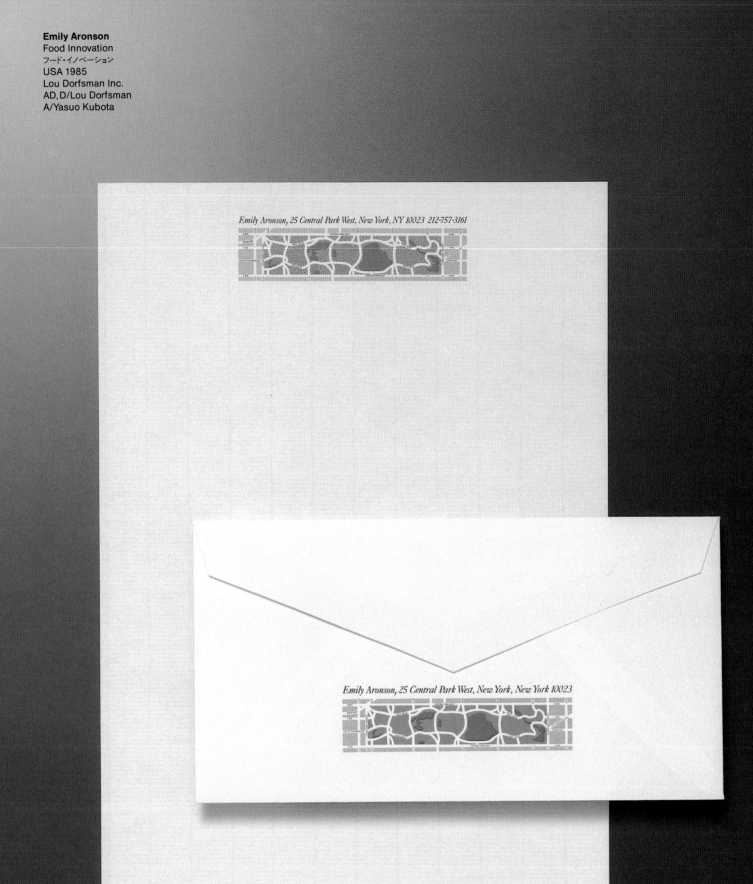

Classic American Foods, Inc.
Food Business
食品会社
USA 1985
Lou Dorfsman Inc.
AD/Lou Dorfsman
D/Lou Dorfsman, Yasuo Kubota
A/Burt Wolf

166 167

Classic American Foods, Inc.  30 Lincoln Plaza, Suite 27N, New York, NY 10023 (212)765-8322

Classic American Foods, Inc.  30 Lincoln Plaza, Suite 27N, New York, New York 10023

The Designers Film Unit
Film Production
映画製作
England 1976
Arnold Schwartzman Productions Inc.
AD,D/Arnold Schwartzman

Dazzling Ace Productions
Film Production
映画製作
England 1978
Arnold Schwartzman Productions Inc.
D/Arnold Schwartzman
A/Victorian Engraving

168 169

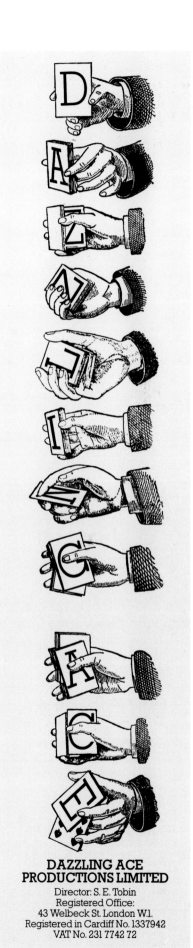

DAZZLING ACE
PRODUCTIONS LIMITED
Director: S. E. Tobin
Registered Office:
43 Welbeck St. London W.1.
Registered in Cardiff No. 1337942
VAT No. 231 7742 72

Fred To
Architect & Aerospace Designer
建築・飛行機製作
England 1982
Pentagram Design
D/John McConnell, John Rushworth

Air Plane Company Limited, 35 South Hill Park, London NW3 2ST, Telephone 01 794 8697

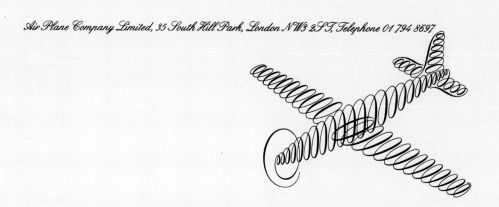

Directors: Frederick E. To, Henry C. Cottrell
Registration number: 1480801 England, Registered Office: Viking House, 17-19 Peterborough Road, Harrow, Middlesex HA1 2XS

Guest & Hughes Film Productions Ltd.
Film Animation Company
アニメーション製作会社
England 1970
Pentagram Design
D/Mervyn Kurlansky

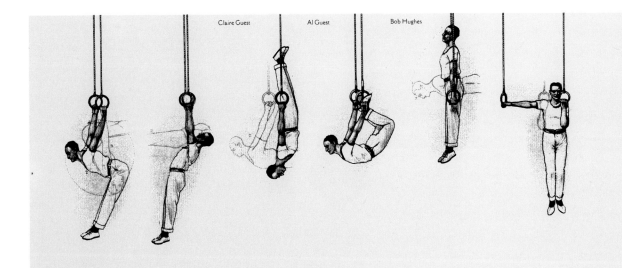

Guest and Hughes Film Productions Ltd 2-3 and Canada House Norfolk Street London WC2

Sharon Grahnquist
Voice Instructor
歌唱指導
USA 1976
The Richards Group
AD, D/Woody Pirtle

Sharon Grahnquist

Sharon Grahnquist

Zimmersmith
Music Production
音楽プロダクション
USA 1979
AD, D, A/Woody Pirtle

172 173

7027 Twin Hills Avenue
Dallas, Texas 75231
(214) 691-1892

ZIMMERSMITH

The Inn at the Tides
Hotel/Resort
ホテル・リゾート施設
USA 1985
Gerald Reis & Company
AD, D, A/Gerald Reis

Caffe Quadro
Caffe & Pizzeria
コーヒー・ピザ店
USA 1985
Gerald Reis & Company
AD, D, A/Gerald Reis

Cimarron Corporation
Feed Lot Operator
畜産会社
USA 1970
The Richards Group
AD, D, A/Woody Pirtle

Stallworth Oil & Gas
Oil and Gas Company
石油・ガス会社
USA 1982
Pirtle Design
AD/Woody Pirtle, Luis Acevedo
D, A/Luis Acevedo

Bedford Press
Art Book Publishers
美術図書出版
USA 1986
Vanderbyl Design
AD, D, A/Michael Vanderbyl

Swedish Goodies
Candy Store
菓子店
USA 1986
Dyer/Khan, Inc.
AD/Rod Dyer
D/Hoi Ping Law

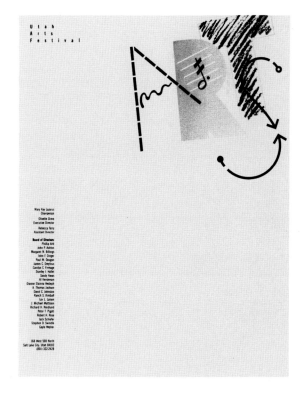

Cynthia Moore
Photographer
写真家
USA 1985
Luci Goodman Studio
D/Luci Goodman

Utah Arts Festival
Yearly Festival of Arts,
Crafts and Music
美術・工芸・音楽フェスティバル
USA 1984
La Pine/O'Very Inc.
AD, D, A/Julia La Pine, Traci O'Very Covey

Visual Research
Visual Reference Research
ヴィジュアル・リサーチ
USA 1985
Arnold Schwartzman Productions Inc.
D/Arnold Schwartzman
A/Victorian Engraving

Café de Paris
Restaurant
レストラン
México 1985
Diseñadores y Consultores
AD, D, A/Alfonso Garoía Reyes

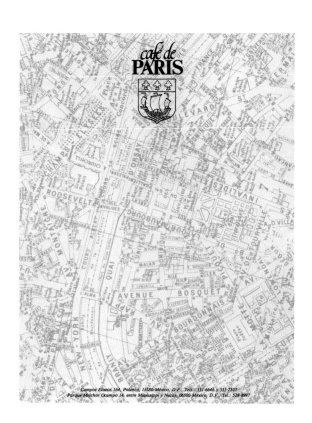

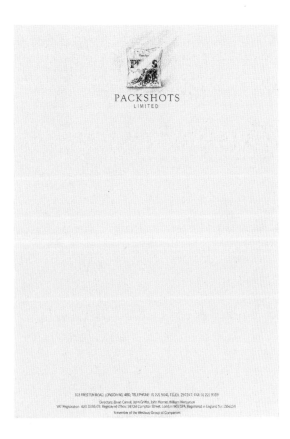

PACKSHOTS
スティール・ショット
England 1985
Michael Peters + Partners
AD/Glenn Tutssel
D/Francis Lovell, Glenn Tutssel
A/Lucy Su

Leslie Jones & Company
Consultant Designers
デザイン・コンサルティング
Australia 1979
Ken Cato Design Company
AD, D/Ken Cato

Sanctuary Cove
Resort and Marina Development
リゾート・海洋開発
Australia 1984
Barrie Tucker Design Pty Ltd.
AD, D/Barrie Tucker
A/Elizabeth Schlooz

The Marine Collection
Marine Specialities Shops
船舶関連用品販売
Australia 1985
Barrie Tucker Design Pty Ltd.
AD, D/Barrie Tucker
A/Elizabeth Schlooz

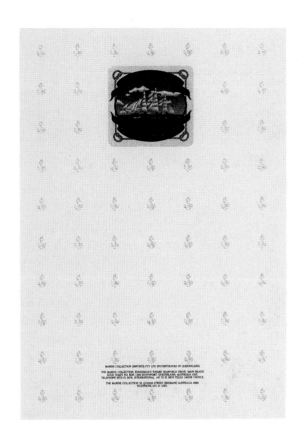

**South Australian Department of
the Arts**
南オーストラリア芸術局
Australia 1982
Barrie Tucker Design Pty Ltd.
AD, D/Barrie Tucker
A/Robert Marshall

Mallscapes
Shopping Mall Landscaping
ショッピング・モール建設
USA 1986
Dennard Creative, Inc.
AD/Bob Dennard   A/Ken Koester
D/Bob Dennard, Ken Koester

Doug Akagi United States

ステーショナリーは，何も書かれていない状態で相手の目に触れることはありません。そこで，私たちはクライアントのタイプライターまたはコンピュータ・プリンターによってつくられる配置線の上に，レターヘッドをデザインします。上下の余白，幅，パラグラフの扱い，それに日付け，冒頭および最後の挨拶と本文との間のスペースのあけ方を指示して，手紙の本文そのものもデザインします。タイプライターのみを使用するクライアントには，手紙の各要素の位置を小さな点（ほとんど見えないくらいの）で指示し，タイピストがタイプしやすいようにします。最後は，下端から3分の2のところに印刷された短い細い線と左端の裁ち切り線を目安に，まず下端がこの線に達するように折りたたみ，さらに上側を折ることで，レターヘッドはきちんと三等分されて折りたたまれるようにします。デザインのプレゼンテーションでは，タイプした手紙を秀明なフィルムに転写してレターヘッドにのせ，そのレターヘッドが使用されたときの様子を見せることにしています。

D.C. Stipp United States

レターヘッドは常にひとつの挑戦です。同一要素を異なった形で展開し，ステーショナリーという限界のなかで作業するのは面白いものですが，同時にその限界を可能なだけ押し拡げ，しかも手紙を書く用紙であることを全うするのは至難の技です。サウス・ストリート祝賀用レターヘッドは行事用として使いますので，この催しの性格に従って，このようなことを念頭に置きつつデザインしました。

Gerry Rosentsieg United States

レターヘッドの重要性は明白です。発信人の名前や住所電話番号以上の何かを，受け取った人に伝えるからです。企業そのものを語ると言ってもいいでしょう。そのためデザイナーは，そのクライアントからのものだとすぐわかり，なおかつそれ以上の何かを語っているようなデザインのレターヘッドをつくることが大切です。仕事の内容を伝達し，また内容にふさわしいデザインであるように気を配らなくてはなりません。逆に言えば，デザイナーがクライアントについての情報をできる限り多く集めなくては，良いレターヘッドがつくれないのです。

特に難しいのは，会社の将来について明確な見とおしが立っていない新しい企業のステーショナリーをデザインするときです。グラフィックや紙，色の選択が企業の性格を決定する場合もままあります。この種のデザインを引き受けるのは，大変難しいことですが，やりがいもまた大きいものです。

Louis Dorfsman United States

デザイナーが，自分自身または親しい友人のためにレターヘッドをデザインする場合には，特別の問題が生じます。ある意味で，個人用ステーショナリーをデザインするにあたって，デザイナーは，いわば"月"に，"究極"のものに，つまり最高の出来ばえで人々を羨ましがらせ，デザイン上の勝利に酔えるようなものに到達しようとします。

しかし，デザイナーが，自分のために自分を超越するようなものを創り出せることはめったにありません。そこで，私たちは安全な場所に引き下がり，自身が批評の的にならぬよう，単に「これは上等の感受性で仕上げたビジネスライクな作品ですが，私の手腕が発揮され，クライアントのために本来の才能が示された作例というわけではありません」と語っているかのような，品のいい，控えめな印刷物を作成することになります。

それでも，友人のためにデザイナーするときには，私はもっとスタイルやコンセプトに工夫のあるものにしようと最善を尽くします。なぜなら，その便せんには他人の名前が印刷されるので，よい結果が得られなかったとき，非難を逃れているような気分になるからです。

Heather Cooper Canada

レターヘッドは，印象的，かつ適切なデザインで，個人や企業のパーソナリティを反映するものでなければなりません。

Marianne Tombaugh United States

ヘイ・エージェンシー（広告代理店）のレターヘッドとCIを考案するにあたっては，基本となる要因がいくつかあげられています。まず，品位とプロフェッショナルを象徴するものであること。堅実な実務上の知識を備えた上で，なおかつ創造性と革新性を発揮する企業を表わすイメージであること。不動産から銀行業，コンピュータ会社から薬用潤滑油会社までと広範囲にわたるクライアントに充分訴えかけるものであること。

一般にグラフィックデザイナーは，デザイン界の動きに遅れまいとする傾向が多分にあります。ですがCIを考案するときには，そのデザインがオリジナルなものであると同時に，時を越えて親しまれるようなマークやロゴとなるよう，特に注意しなくてはなりません。レターヘッドやCIの寿命は，そのまま企業の寿命でもあります。新しくやり直したり，手直ししたりするような必要があってはならないのです。デザイナーが，デザインの歴史やサイクルを意識しながら色，形，文字，紙を選択しないと，すぐに時代とそぐわないものになってしまいます。

Richard Moore United States

レターヘッドのデザインも，他のグラフィックデザインとあまり変わるところはありません。個人からの依頼であろうと大企業からの発注であろうと，そのデザインはクライアントの性格を視覚的に表現するものでなくてはならないからです。しかしデザインによっては，既製の印刷物を越える効果をあげることも可能です。さらにデザイナーは，そのレターヘッドを使用する人が，タイプで打ち込む文字のフォーマットも，デザインの一要素として考慮しなくてはなりません。この本でもわかるように，何も書かれていないレターヘッドは美しいけれども，不完全なものなのです。デザイナーやクライアントの秘書以外は，タイプされていないレターヘッドを見ることはほとんどありません。タイプされるであろう文字のフォーマットもデザインの要素として扱えば，さらに効果的な印象を見る者に与えます。

Marilyn Worseldine United States

私の名字はとても難しいスペルなのです。私は，これまでに，信じられないような間違い方をした私あての手紙を集めています。
こうしたミススペルをレターヘッドに取り入れたら面白いなと思っています。住所のすぐ上に，正しいスペルを別の色で印刷したりして…。
Worselwhat?（ウォーセル，何ですって?）

Cynthia H. Marsh United States

自分ではレターヘッドとステーショナリーはたびたび変えるべきだと思っています。視覚的なインパクトを，見る人に与えることで，現時点の私の生活をつくりだしているさまざまな影響を表現しなくては，と考えているのです。

Tommy Steele United States

グラフィックデザインのなかでも，レターヘッドと名刺のデザインは，私たち自身の宣伝材料にもなります。イメージ・メーカーで，私たちがだれなのかを，見る人に伝えてくれる題材だからでしょう。こうしたアイデンティティ商品をもっとクライアントに販売していく必要がありそうです。企業の顔は，企業が売る商品と同じように大事なものです。
残念ながら私たちがデザインする実験的なレターヘッドは，ほとんどが自分たちで使うものばかりです。それが私たちデザイナーの仕事でもあるわけですが……。実験的なデザインを見せて，人々のデザイン・レベルを上げるのも，大事なことです。それに，古いのを使いきったときには新しくデザインし直すいいわけにもなります。いつも，新しいものを追いかけていなければなりませんから。

Miranda Moss United States

私たちがデザインするレターヘッドは，CIのトータル・プログラムの一部となっています。商業通信文が主として企業イメージを伝える役割を果たしている場合，あるいは潜在的な顧客に到達するための最初のマーケティング手段となっている場合など，企業によってさまざまです。私たちの経験では，カラーのシンボルやグラフィックを使った方が，注目を集める上に鮮明な印象を残しています。

Cary Staples United States

レターヘッドは通常，企業にとって，外部の人から内側をうかがわれる最初の機会となりますから，企業アイデンティティの要素として非常に重要なものです。レターヘッドは単に住所と名前が印刷された1枚の紙ではなく，企業が外の世界とのコミュニケーションに用いる系統だった方法のひとつなのです。
視覚的な第一印象が大切ですが，機能的な考慮が充分になされていない場合には，その視覚的な印象も薄いものになってしまいます。レターヘッドは，機能的で使いやすいものでなければなりません。そのために考慮されなければならないことがいくつかあります。まず，レイアウト上の考慮については，その会社が使用している各種の書式とワードプロセッサーなどについて知る必要があります。次に，在庫の面で，郵便物についての体系化が行なわれている場合，指定された用紙の充分な供給が必要です。字体については，使用されているタイプライターまたはプリンターの字体と調和するものを選ばなければなりません。さらに，法律的また予算上の制約も考慮する必要があります。
その会社の実体を分析するとともに，企業理念といったようなものも分析してみて，会社が外部に対して示したいと望んでいる独自性を発見し，それらを実務的考慮と融合させることが，適切かつ独自性のあるデザインを創造するための第一歩といえるでしょう。

April Greiman United States

個人が使うためのレターヘッドをデザインする……いちばん難しい依頼です。
業務用のレターヘッドは……ほとんどの場合，個性のかけらもなく，重要な情報やメッセージを伝えようとしても，印刷上の問題でその機会を失うことがあります。
コンピュータ時代のレターヘッドは……ラフスケッチなどをコンピュータで処理します。

Akagi Design
Graphic Design
グラフィックデザイン
USA 1984
Akagi Design
AD, D/Doug Akagi

AKAGI DESIGN

17 Osgood Place

San Francisco

California

9 4 1 3 3

415 397-4668

McCoy & McCoy
Design Consultants
デザイン・コンサルティング
USA 1978
McCoy & McCoy
AD, D/Katherine & Michael McCoy

180 181

McCoy & McCoy

Design consultants

500 Lone Pine Road
Box 801

Bloomfield Hills
MI 48013 USA

313 642.9570
313 645.3336

Bottoni Design
Graphic Design
グラフィックデザイン
USA 1985
Bottoni Design
D/Joseph Bottoni

2311
Park
Avenue
Cincinnati
Ohio
45206

Phone
861 0544

Graphic
Design

Works
Graphic, Exhibit,
and Environmental Design
グラフィック・展示・環境デザイン
USA 1980
Works
AD/Godard, van Djik, Tevonian
D/Tevonian, van Djik, Godard

182 183

design group   **Works**

45 West 27th Street
New York, NY 10001

212 **696 1666**

partners

Keith Godard
Stephanie Tevonian
Hans van Dijk

Harry Murphy + Friends
Design Office
グラフィックデザイン
USA 1985
AD, D/Harry Murphy

Harry Murphy + Friends
225 Miller Avenue
Mill Valley, CA 94941
Telephone 415 383-8586

Corporate Identity
Print Graphics
Packaging
Advertising
Exhibition Design
Architectural Graphics
Signing Systems
Interior Design
Color Consulting
Environmental Art

Minale, Tattersfield & Partners Ltd. ·
Design Consultancy
デザイン・コンサルティング
England 1964
Minale, Tattersfield & Partners, Ltd.
AD, D, A/Marcello Minale,
Brian Tattersfield

Minale, Tattersfield & Partners Limited

Kurt Wirth
Graphic Designer
グラフィックデザイン
Switzerland 1984
Kurt Wirth
AD, D, A/Kurt Wirth

kurt wirth   grafiker designer   ch-3006 bern
                                                   bürglenstrasse 21
                              agi swb sgv   t   031   44 63 88

Worseldine Graphic Design
Graphic Design
グラフィックデザイン
USA 1985
Worseldine Graphic Design
AD, D/Marilyn Worseldine

Tommy Steele
Design
デザイン
USA 1984
Steeleworks Design
AD, D, A/Tommy Steele

1041 NORTH MᶜCADDEN PLACE, LOS ANGELES, CALIFORNIA 90038 · (213) 465·4075

Glenn Parsons
Design, Lettering, Illustration
デザイン・レタリング・イラストレーション
USA 1985
Glenn Parsons Design
AD, D, A/Glenn Parsons

188 189

GLENN PARSONS DESIGN

1548 Eighteenth Street 102

SANTA MONICA CALIFORNIA 90404

213 828 0751

☐ INVOICE

☐ ESTIMATE

TO:

DATE:

INVOICE NUMBER:

CLIENT'S P.O. NUMBER:

ASSIGNMENT DESCRIPTION:

DESIGN:

ILLUSTRATION:

MATERIALS:

PRODUCTION:

LETTERING:

TYPE:

STATS:

ROUGHS:

COMPS:

OTHER:

DESIGN

TOTAL:

SALES TAX:

TOTAL FEE:

TERMS: TOTAL AMOUNT DUE IN THIRTY DAYS.

THANK YOU:

4

Quay & Gray
Lettering & Graphic Designers
レタリング・グラフィックデザイン
England 1983
Quay & Gray
D/David Quay
A/Paul Gray

Kangas Design Associates
Industrial Design
インダストリアルデザイン
Canada
Kangas Design Associates
AD/Mark Cryns

190 191

KANGAS
Design Associates

Industrial Design

Product Development

Prototyping

Product Illustration

Box 271 Station A
Willowdale, Ontario
M2N 5S9

Woody Pirtle
Designer
デザイナー
USA 1973
AD, D, A/Woody Pirtle

WOODY PIRTLE

**Katsu Kimura & Packaging
Direction Co., Ltd.**
Package Design Studio
パッケージ・デザイン
Japan 1985
Katsu Kimura & Packaging
Direction Co., Ltd.
D/Katsu Kimura

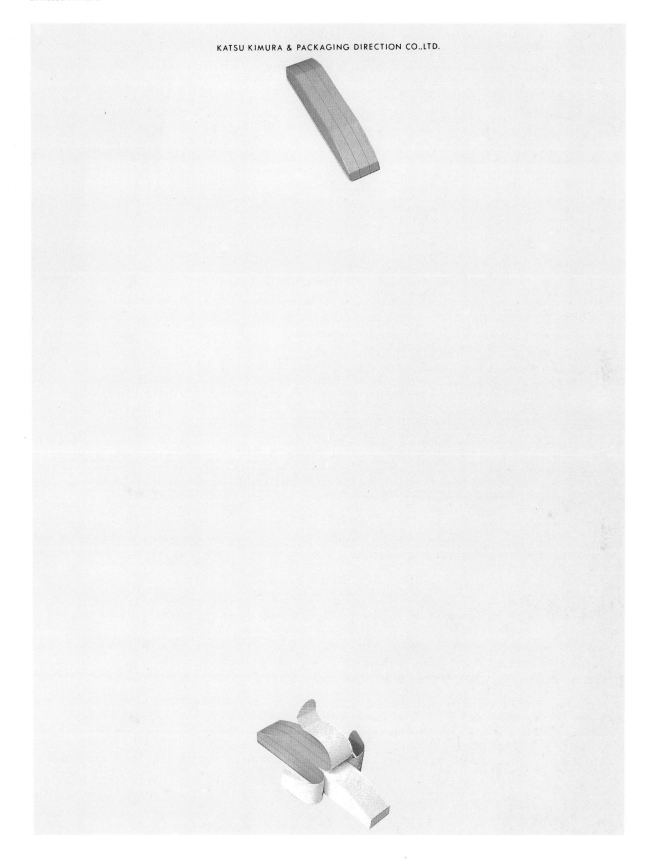

KATSU KIMURA & PACKAGING DIRECTION CO.,LTD.

**Katsu Kimura & Packaging
Direction Co., Ltd.**
Package Design Studio
パッケージ・デザイン
Japan 1985
Katsu Kimura & Packaging
Direction Co., Ltd.
D/Katsu Kimura

KATSU KIMURA & PACKAGING DIRECTION CO.,LTD.

The Hay Agency, Inc.
Avertising Agency
広告代理業
USA 1983
The Hay Agency
AD, D, A/Marianne Tombaugh

Paul Davis Studio
Illustration
イラストレーション
USA 1984
Paul Davis Studio
AD/Paul Davis
D/Paul Davis, José Conde

Paul Davis Studio

14 East 4th Street, New York, NY 10012, (212) 420-8789

Paul Davis Studio 14 East 4th Street, New York, NY 10012

Paul Davis Studio

14 East 4th Street, New York, NY 10012, (212) 420-8789

Skolos, Wedell & Raynor, Inc.
Graphic Design and Photography
グラフィックデザイン・写真
USA 1985
Skolos, Wedell & Raynor, Inc.
D/Nancy Skolos

Rick Eiber Design
Graphic Design
グラフィックデザイン
USA 1984
Rick Eiber Design
AD, D, A／Rick Eiber

196 197

Seitz Yamamoto Moss
Design Office
デザイン・オフィス
USA 1982
Seitz Yamamoto Moss
AD, D/Hideki Yamamoto, Miranda Moss

Owens/Lutter
Graphic Design
グラフィックデザイン
USA
AD, D, A/Chris Owens

198 199

Kit & Linda Hinrichs
Design
デザイン
USA 1977
Pentagram Design
AD/Kit Hinrichs

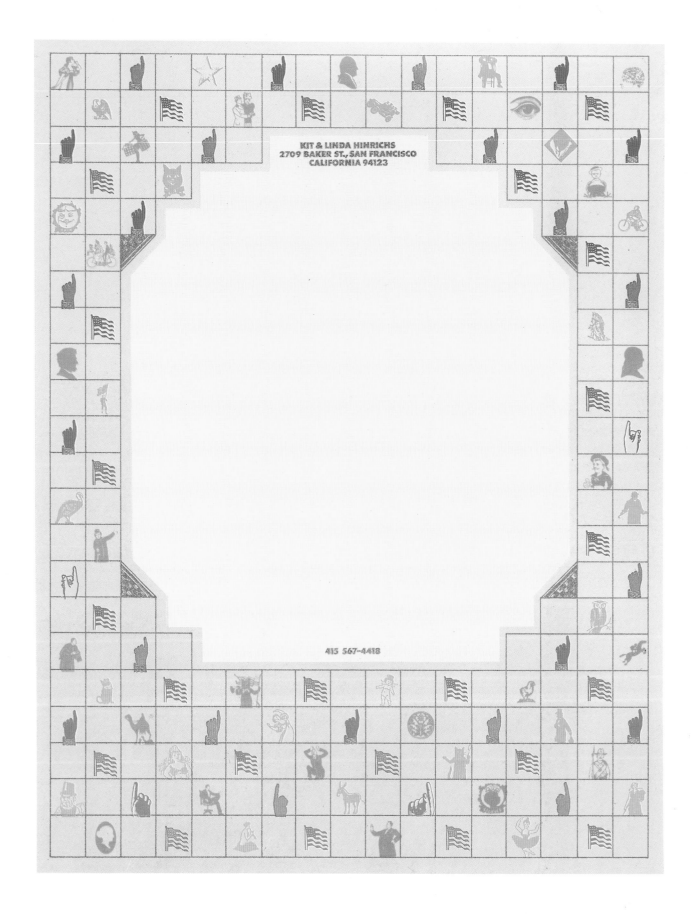

KIT & LINDA HINRICHS
2709 BAKER ST., SAN FRANCISCO
CALIFORNIA 94123

415 567-4418

Glen Iwasaki
Graphic Designer
グラフィックデザイン
USA
D/Glen Iwasaki

200 201

Glen
Iwasaki

3535
Corinth
Avenue

Los Angeles
California
90066

telephone:
213
297-3681

Glen Iwasaki
Graphic Designer
グラフィックデザイン
USA
D/Glen Iwasaki

Oswaldo Miranda
Design Studio
デザイン・スタジオ
Brazil 1985
Miran Studio
AD, D, A/Oswaldo Miranda

Oswaldo Miranda (Miran)

Comunicação Visual
Editorial
Embalagens/Marcas
Ilustrações

Oswaldo Miranda (Miran)

Oswaldo Miranda (Miran)

Comunicação Visual
Editorial
Embalagens/Marcas
Ilustrações

Oswaldo Miranda (Miran)

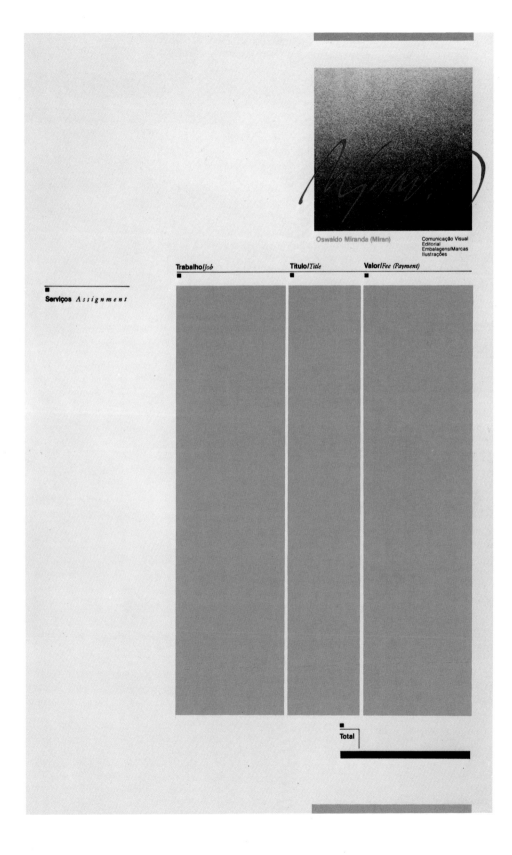

Oswaldo Miranda (Miran)

Comunicação Visual
Editorial
Embalagens/Marcas
Ilustrações

Serviços *Assignment*

Trabalho/*Job*	**Título/***Title*	**Valor/***Fee (Payment)*

Total

Laughlin/Winkler
Graphic Designers
グラフィックデザイナー
USA 1981
Laughlin/Winkler
AD, D/Mark Laughlin, Ellen Winkler

April Greiman
Design & Consulting
デザイン・コンサルティング
USA 1982
April Greiman Inc.
AD, D, A/April Greiman

April Greiman
April Greiman
Incorporated

213 / *227-1222*

620 Moulton Avenue

#211

Los Angeles

California 90031

April Greiman
Design & Consulting
デザイン・コンサルティング
USA 1982
April Greiman Inc.
AD, D, A/April Greiman

Harry Metzler
Graphic Designer
グラフィックデザイナー
Austria 1986
Harry Metzler
AD, D, A/Harry Metzler

Brand 774
6867 Schwarzenberg
Austria / Europe
Telephone 0 5512 34 94

Takenobu Igarashi International
Design Consulting Firm
デザイン・コンサルティング会社
USA 1985
Igarashi Studio
AD/Takenobu Igarashi
D/Debi Shimamoto

206 207

Noriko Moore
Graphic Designer
グラフィックデザイン
USA
Muir Cornelius Moore
D/Noriko & Richard Moore

Date

Noriko Moore

Mr. John Smith
Title
Company Name
Street Address
City, State, Zip Code

21 Bond Street

New York, NY 10012

Tel 212 673-4965

Dear John,

Noriko Moore letterheads have been designed for use with the
particular typing format demonstrated here. All typing is flush
left, with no indentations. Paragraphs are separated by a line
space between them. Writer/typist, enclosure and copy information
is typed as low as possible on the page, as indicated.

Note that two small dots have been printed to indicate the
positioning of the date/ address information and body of the letter.
A similar dot will be found on the envelope.

Sincerely yours,

Name
Title

JS/nm
Encl.
cc;Mr. Robert Jones, Mr. David White

Weisz & Yang Inc.
Graphic Design
グラフィックデザイン
USA 1984
Weisz & Yang Inc.
AD,D/Larry Yang

208 209

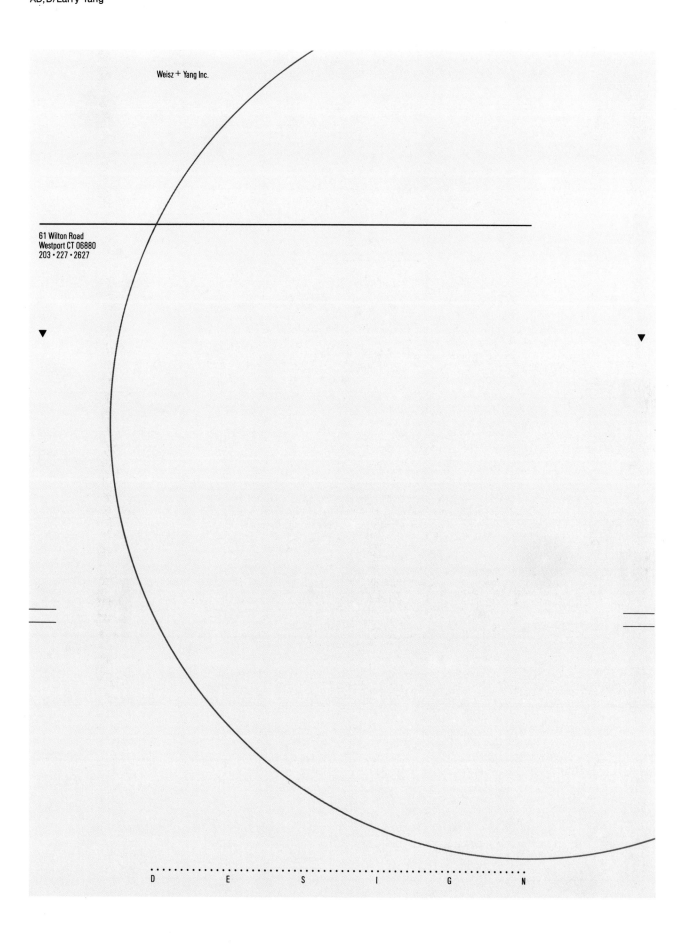

Weisz + Yang Inc.

61 Wilton Road
Westport CT 06880
203 · 227 · 2627

D   E   S   I   G   N

Michael Patrick Cronan Design, Inc.
グラフィックデザイン
USA 1986
Michael Patrick Cronan Design, Inc.
AD/Michael Patrick Cronan, Linda Lawler
D/Linda Lawler

Michael Patrick Cronan Design, Inc.
グラフィックデザイン
USA 1986
Michael Patrick Cronan Design, Inc.
AD/Michael Patrick Cronan, Linda Lawler
D/Linda Lawler

Sussman/Prejza & Co.
Environmental Design
環境デザイン
USA 1986
Sussman/Prejza & Co.
AD/Deborah Sussman
D/Luci Goodman

Sussman/Prejza & Company, Inc.

1651 18th Street

Santa Monica

California 90404

213 829 3337

Scott Cuyler

Mark Nelsen

Paul Prejza

Deborah Sussman

FAX 213 829 7267

Russel Halfhide
Graphic Design and Illustration
グラフィックデザイン・イラストレーション
Trinidad & Tobago 1983
D, A/Russel Halfhide

The Weller Institute
For the Cure of Design, Inc.
Graphic Design
グラフィックデザイン
USA 1986
The Weller Institute
for the Cure of Design, Inc.
AD, D/Don Weller

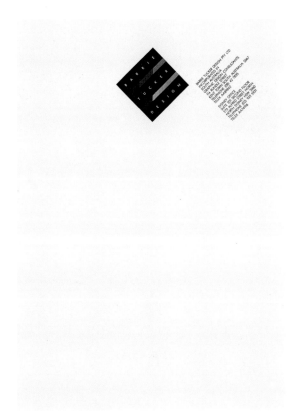

Cary Staples Graphic Design
グラフィックデザイナー
USA 1985
Cary Staples Graphic Design
AD, D/Cary Staples

Barry Tucker Design Pty Ltd.
Graphic Design Consultancy
グラフィックデザイン・コンサルティング
Australia 1985
Barry Tucker Design Pty Ltd.
AD, D/Barrie Tucker
A/Mark Janetzki

**Arnold Schwartzman
Productions Inc.**
Film Production and Graphic Design
映画製作・グラフィックデザイン
USA 1980
Arnold Schwartzman Productions Inc.
AD, D, A/Arnold Schwartzman

The Gene Federico Family
Paper Company Promotional Letterhead
紙会社のプロモーション用レターヘッド
USA 1972
Gene Federico
AD/Gene Federico, Herb Lubalin
D, A/Gene Federico
C/Gilbert Paper Company

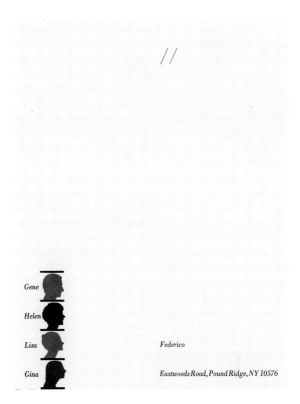

Theo Dimson Design Inc.
Graphic Design
グラフィックデザイン
Canada 1983
D/Theo Dimson
A/Theo Dimson, Ken Jackson

Morteza Momayez
Graphic Designer
グラフィックデザイナー
Iran 1985
Morteza Momayez
AD, D, A/Morteza Momayez

Cynthia Marsh
Photo and Illustration
写真・イラストレーション
USA 1985
Cynthia Marsh
AD, D, A/Cynthia Marsh

William Deere
Graphic Designer
グラフィックデザイン
USA 1985
AD/Katherine McCoy
A/William Deere

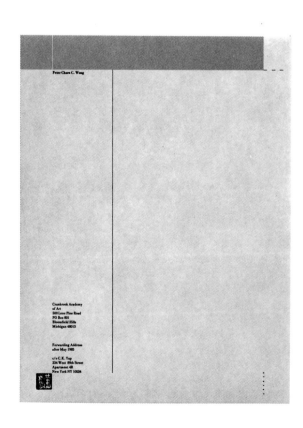

Peter Charn C. Wong
Graphic Designer
グラフィックデザイン
USA 1985
AD/Katherine McCoy
D/Peter Charn C. Wong

Igarashi Studio
Design Firm
デザイン会社
Japan 1985
Igarashi Studio
AD/Takenobu Igarashi
D/Hiromi Nakata

Robert Miles Runyan & Associates
Graphic Design
グラフィックデザイン
USA
Robert Miles Runyan & Associates
AD/Robert Miles Runyan
D/Stephan Sieler

Michael Manwaring
Graphic Designer
グラフィックデザイナー
USA
The Office of Michael Marwaring
AD, D, A/Michael Manwaring

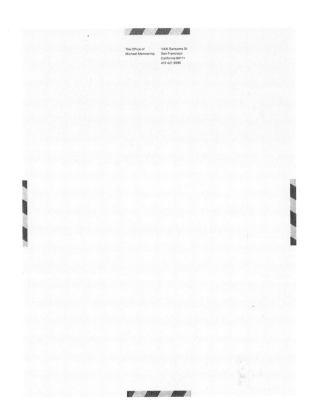

La Pine/O'Very Inc.
Design Firm
デザイン会社
USA 1984
La Pine/O'Very Inc.
AD, D, A/Julia La Pine, Traci O'Very Covey

Gerald Reis & Company
Graphic Design
グラフィックデザイン
USA 1982
Gerald Reis & Company
AD, D, A/Gerald Reis

Jacques Garamond
Graphic Designer
グラフィックデザイン
France 1968
Garamond
AD, D, A/Jacques N. Garamond

Pat Hansen Design
Graphic Design
グラフィックデザイン
USA 1984
Pat Hansen Design
D/Pat Hansen, Paula Richards,
Jesse Doquilo

Dennis Doherty Design Ltd.
Graphic Design
グラフィックデザイン
Canada
Dennis Doherty Design Ltd.
AD, D/Dennis Doherty

Medina Design
Graphic Design
グラフィックデザイン
Canada 1980
Medina Design
AD, D, A/Fernando Medina

Giulio Cittato
Designer
グラフィックデザイン
Italy 1971
Giulio Cittato
AD, D/Giulio Cittato

The Cartoon Gallery
Graphic Design Studio
グラフィックデザイン・スタジオ
England
D/Mel Calman

216 217

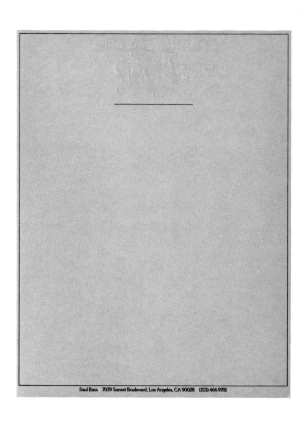

Saul Bass/Herb Yager & Associates
Graphic Design
グラフィックデザイン
USA 1979
D, A/Saul Bass

Heather Cooper
Artist & Graphic Designer
グラフィックデザイナー
Canada 1983
Heather Cooper Illustration & Design
D/Heather Cooper
A/Diane Mellor

SWEDEN

Olle Eksell Design
Hedinsgatan 15
11533 Stockholm
Sweden
101

SWITZERLAND

Geissbühler, Karl Domenig
Theaterstrasse 10
8001 Zürich
Switzerland
40

**Gottschalk + Ash
International**
Sonnhaldenstrasse 3
8032 Zürich
Switzerland
55, 117

**Graphis Press
Corporation**
Walter Herdeg
107 Dufourstrasse
CH-8008 Zürich
Switzerland
120

Bruno Monguzzi
6866 Meride
Switzerland
79

Oberholzer Tagli Cevio
Mr. Sabina Oberholzer
Grafico ASG
CH 6675 Cevio Switzerland
Renato Tagli
Grafico ASG
CH 6574 Vira Gamb.
Switzerland
81, 118, 136

Odermatt & Tissi
Schipfe 45
8001 Zürich Switzerland
91, 118

Kurt Wirth
Burglenstrasse 21
3006 Bern
Switzerland
110, 186

UNITED STATES

Akagi Design
17 Osgood Place
San Francisco, CA 94133
USA
125, 180

Apple Creative Services
Tom Suiter
20525 Mariani Avenue
Cupertino, CA 95014
USA
112

Bottoni Design
2311 Park Avenue
Cincinnati, Ohio 45206
USA
54, 182

**Saul Bass/Herb Yager &
Associates**
7039 Sunset Blvd.
Los Angeles, CA 90028
USA
57, 104, 105, 217

**Chermayeff & Geismar
Associates**
15 East 26th Street
New York, NY 10010
USA
116, 122, 123

**Michael Patrick Cronan
Design, Inc.**
One Zoe
San Francisco, CA 94107
USA
35, 61, 73, 210

Paul Davis Studio
14 East 4th Street
New York, NY 10012
USA
22, 195

**Rudolph de Harak &
Assoc., Inc.**
320 West 13th Street
New York, NY 10014
USA
91, 117

William Deere
500 Lone Pine Road
Box 801
Bloomfield Hills
MI 48013 USA
214

Dennard Creative, Inc.
13601 Preston Road
Carillon Tower
East Dallas, Texas 75240
USA
177

Lou Dorfsman Inc.
51 West 52 Street
New York, NY 10019
USA
53, 166, 167

Dyer/Kahn Inc.
5550 Wilshire Blvd.
Suite 301
Los Angles, CA 90036
USA
16, 59, 162, 163, 175

Rick Eiber Design
3019 Northwest Sixty Fifth
Seattle, Washington 98107
USA
84, 144, 147, 197

Esprit
900 Minnesota St.
San Francisco, CA 94107
USA
106, 107

Gene Federico
655 Madison Avenue
New York, NY 10021
USA
47, 55, 213

Mike Fink Graphic Design
4434 Matilija Avenue
Sherman Oaks, CA 91423
USA
58, 72

John Follis & Associates
2124 W. Venice Blvd.
L.A., CA 90016
USA
61

Gonda Design, Inc.
241 West 23rd Street
New York, NY 10011
USA
21, 98, 116

Luci Goodman Studio
918 Third Street
No.8
Santa Monica, CA 90403
USA
175

April Greiman Inc.
620 Moulton Ave. 211
Los Angeles, CA 90031
USA
64, 65, 66, 67, 90, 205

Pat Hansen Design
618 Second Ave.,
Suite 1080
Seattle, Washington 98104
USA
78, 216

The Hay Agency, Inc.
2121 San Jacinto Street
San Jacinto Tower
Suite 800
Dallas, Texas 75201
USA
194

Jim Heimann Design
618 S. Western #205
Los Angeles, CA 90005
USA
146

Wayne Hunt Design, Inc
87 North Raymond Avenue
Suite 215
Pasadena, CA 91103
USA
45

Images
126

Glen Iwasaki
3535 Corinth Avenue
Los Angeles, CA 90066
USA
52, 201

Krause & Young, Inc.
703 McKinney
The Brewery
Suite 444
Dallas, Texas 75202
USA
20, 139

La Pine/O'Very Inc.
701 East South Temple
Salt Lake City
Utah 84102
USA
23, 142, 143, 175, 215

Laughlin/Winkler
205 A Street
Boston MA 02210
USA
33, 85, 86, 87, 204

James Leinhart Design
58 West Huron
Chicago, IL 60610
USA
29

**The Office of Michael
Manwaring**
1005 Sansome Street
San Francisco, CA 94111
USA
24, 68, 215

Cynthia Marsh
4434 Matilija Ave.
Sherman Oaks, CA 91423
USA
214

**McCoy & McCoy Design
Consultants**
500 Lone Pine Road
Box 801
Bloomfield Hills
MI 48013 USA
57, 181

Tomoko Miho Co.
1045 Fifth Ave.
New York 10028
USA
30

Muir Cornelius Moore
21 Bond Street
New York, NY 10012
USA
208

Harry Murphy + Friends
225 Miller Avenue
Mill Valley, CA 94941
USA
32, 59, 184

**Owens/Lutter Graphic
Design**
Christine Owens
3080 Olcott St.
Suite 200C
Santa Clara, CA
USA
199

Glenn Parsons Design
1548 Eighteenth St. 102
Santa Monica, CA 90404
USA
138, 189

Pate International
45 Houston Street
San Francisco, CA 94133
USA
28

Pentagram Design
212 Fifth Avenue
New York, NY 10010
USA
74, 102

Pentagram Design
620 Davis Street
San Francisco, CA 94111
USA
44, 129, 200

Pirtle Design
4528 McKinney Avenue
Suite 104
Dallas, Texas 75205
USA
*60, 108, 127, 128, 131,
172, 173, 174, 192*

Design Group Works
45 West 27th Street
New York, NY 10001
USA
34, 121, 183

Peter Charn C. Wong
Cranbrook Academy of Art
500 Lone Pine Road
P.O. Box 801
Bloomfield Hills MI 48013
USA
214

**Worseldine Graphic
Design**
1231 30 Street
Northwest Washington DC
20007
USA
141, 187

**Bunny Zaruba Graphic
Design**
19 Booker Avenue
Sausalito, CA 94965
USA
80, 90

Zender & Associates
2311 Park Avenue
Cincinnati OH 45206
USA
76, 77

WEST GERMANY

Mendell & Oberer
Widenmeyerstrasse 12
8000 München 22
W. Germany
54, 159

BK Wiese Visual Design
Allhornweg 7
2000 Hamburg 67
W. Germany
82, 83

WEST INDIES

Russel Halfhide
Graphic Design/Illustration
28 Angelina Street
St. James
Port of Spain, Trinidad
West Indies
212

LETTERHEADS
世界のレターヘッド

1986年12月25日	初版第1刷発行
1987年 8 月25日	第2刷発行
1988年 3 月25日	第3刷発行

定価	9,800円
編者	五十嵐威暢ⓒ
発行者	久世利郎
印刷所	凸版印刷株式会社
製本所	凸版印刷株式会社
発行所	株式会社グラフィック社
	〒102 東京都千代田区九段北1-9-12
	電話03(263)4318　振替・東京3-114345
	落丁・乱丁はお取替え致します。

監修	五十嵐威暢
監修補佐	中村善郎
アートディレクション	五十嵐威暢
カバー・デザイン	寺田朝治
レイアウト	中村善郎
撮影	伊奈英次
	ロベルト・カーラ(p106,107)
翻訳	株式会社エヌシービー開発センター
写植印字	外語印刷株式会社
	三和写真工芸株式会社
印刷・製本	凸版印刷株式会社
グラフィック社編集担当	奥田政喜
	スコット・ブラウス

ISBN4-7661-0408-0 C3070 ¥9800E